BIBLE CRAFTS ON A SHOESTRING BUDGET

Paper Plates & Cups

Rainbow Publishers

BIBLE CRAFTS ON A SHOESTRING BUDGET

Paper Plates & Cups

Pamela J. Kuhn

BIBLE CRAFTS ON A SHOESTRING BUDGET/PAPER PLATES & CUPS
©2002 by Rainbow Publishers, third printing
ISBN 1-58411-002-3
Rainbow reorder# RB38011

Rainbow Publishers
P.O. Box 261129
San Diego, CA 92196

Illustrator: Chuck Galey
Editor: Christy Allen

Printed in the United States of America

Table of Contents

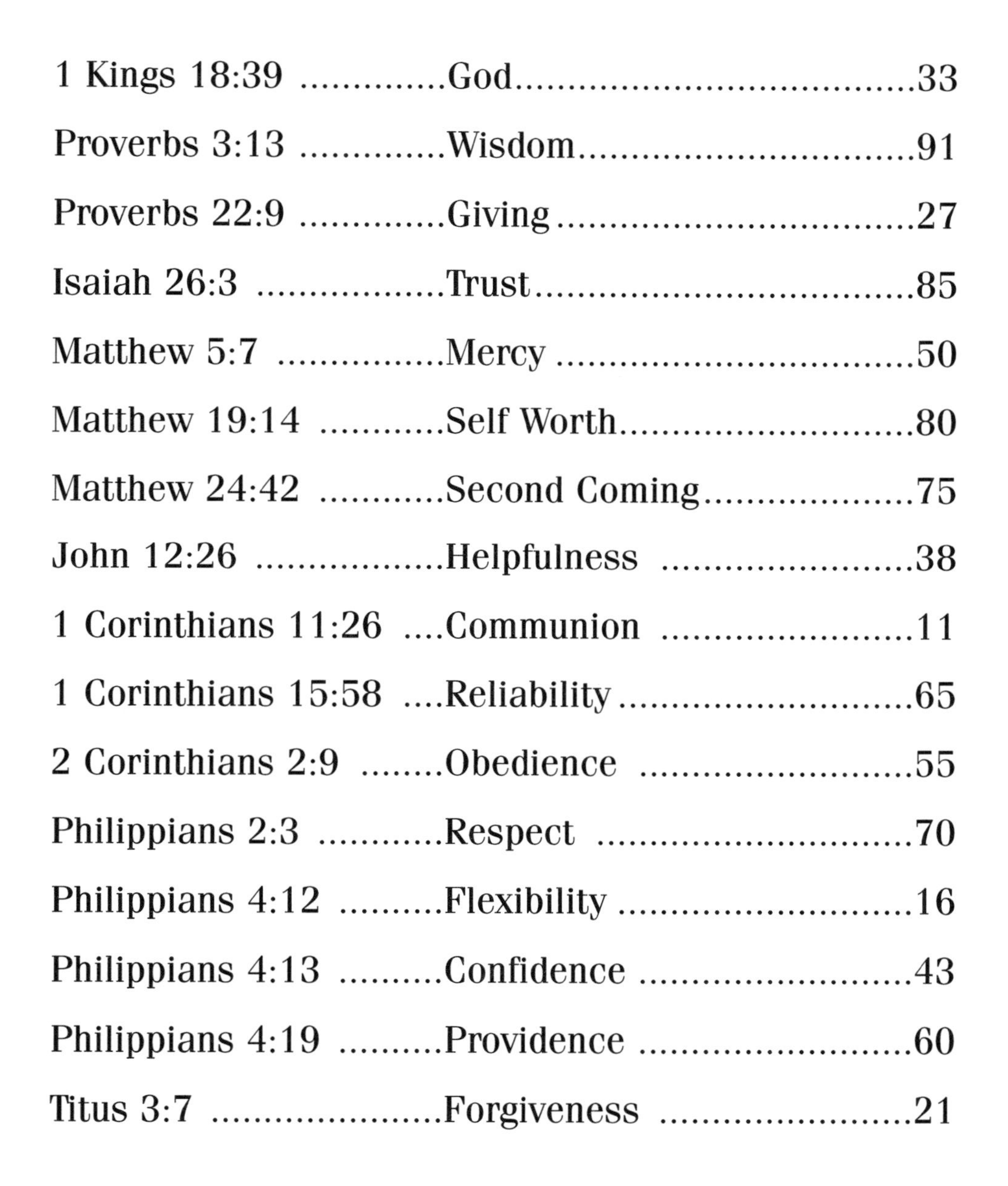

Memory Verse Index

Introduction

Do your students enjoy making crafts? No doubt! Next question: Are you looking for crafts that are fun and inexpensive? *Bible Crafts on a Shoestring Budget* is your answer. Based on everyday items like paper plates and cups, these crafts are designed to get kids excited about the Lord. And with the reproducible patterns and easy instructions, you can focus your energy on teaching the Bible.

Each chapter begins with a Bible story, which is matched with a memory verse and discussion starters. After you tell the story, there are two craft projects that will help students retain the lesson's message and learn the memory verse.

This book is intended to make class time enjoyable for the teacher, too. Each craft includes:

What You Need: a materials list

Before Class: ideas for pre-craft preparation

What to Do: a step-by-step guide to completing the craft

What to Say: talking points to help you relate the lesson

Adapt these lessons to fit your Sunday school or vacation Bible school students. Use them in your Christian day school art classes or in your home. You will be reinforcing Scripture and stories from the Bible — the greatest book ever written — and creatively making a permanent impression on the hearts of your children.

Communion

Memory Verse

Whenever you eat this bread and drink this cup, you proclaim the Lord's death until he comes. ~**1 Corinthians 11:26**

Remembering Jesus

Based on Matthew 26:17-30

Jesus had sent Peter and John to Jerusalem to prepare for the Passover. He knew the time was near for His death and that this would be the last meal all 12 disciples would have together.

When Jesus and the other disciples came to the place of the feast, He was pleased with the good job the two men had done in preparing it.

The disciples all ignored the basin of water with the fresh towel waiting to clean their feet. No one was eager for the job. Jesus got up and went to the basin. He wrapped the towel around His waist and carried the basin to James.

The disciples watched as Jesus knelt in front of James and gently washed his feet, drying them on the towel. By the time it was Peter's turn, he couldn't keep still any longer. "No, Jesus, I don't want You to kneel and wash my feet," he said.

"Then you will not be a part of Me, Peter," said Jesus quietly.

Peter thrust his feet out toward the basin. "Wash them then, and not just my feet but my hands and head as well!"

When Jesus was done He explained, "I have washed your feet as an example, to teach you that you are all equal. No one is greater than another, therefore be humble and kind to each other."

Then Jesus returned to the table. He picked up the bread, blessed it, broke it in pieces and passed it to His disciples. "Take this and eat it," He told them. "This is My body."

Then He blessed the wine and passed it around. "Drink this," He said, "for this is My blood."

"I won't always be with you," Jesus told His disciples. "Make a practice of this communion that we have had. Remember Me when you do this."

For Discussion

1. When you do certain things do they remind you of someone? Does the smell of flowers remind you of your mother? Does the smell of wood chips remind you of your father's workshop or the taste of fresh bread remind you of your grandmother?

2. How does communion remind us of Jesus?

A Framed Picture

Making a sparkling picture of communion will be a reminder of the special time we put aside to remember Jesus.

What You Need

- ⇨ communion picture on page 13
- ⇨ paper plates
- ⇨ scissors
- ⇨ construction paper
- ⇨ glue
- ⇨ crayons
- ⇨ hair spray
- ⇨ glitter

Before Class

Duplicate the communion picture on page 13 for each child. Make a sample picture so the children can see the finished craft.

What To Do

1. Have the children cut out the center of a paper plate.
2. Show how to cut a construction paper circle ½" larger than the piece cut from the paper plate.
3. Give each child a communion picture to color and cut out.
4. Assist as the students lightly spray the colored picture with hair spray, then allow them to sprinkle the picture with glitter.
5. Instruct the children to glue the construction paper circle to the back of the frame.
6. Assist in gluing the picture to the front of the construction paper.

SAY

Look how special your picture is! When you look at it, remember what Jesus did to give you eternal life.

Whenever you eat this bread and drink this cup, you proclaim the Lord's death until he comes. 1Corinthians 11:26

Pencil Holder of Thanks

This Pencil Holder will remind your children what Jesus did for them each time they use it.

What You Need

- ⇨ cross, tomb and sun from page 15
- ⇨ clear cups
- ⇨ markers
- ⇨ construction paper
- ⇨ hole punch
- ⇨ glue
- ⇨ scissors
- ⇨ pencils

Before Class

Duplicate the cross, tomb and sun from page 15. Make a sample pencil holder so the students can see the finished craft.

What To Do

1. Give each child a sun, cross and tomb to color and cut out.
2. Instruct the children to glue the sun, cross and tomb to the cup.
3. Allow the children to use a hole punch to create confetti from the construction paper, then glue it all around the cup.
4. Assist the children in running glue around the rim of the cup. They should fit the decorated cup inside another clear, undecorated cup. The glue at the rim will hold the two cups together. The outside cup will serve as a clear protective layer over the items that were glued to the first cup.
5. Give the children a pencil for the holder.

SAY

Jesus died for you, (say child's name). He died for you, too, (say another name). He died for all of us. When you use a pencil from your holder, take a minute to remember what Jesus did for you.

Flexibility

Memory Verse

I have learned the secret of being content in any and every situation.

~Philippians 4:12

A Change of Address

Based on Daniel 1:1-21

The kings of Judah were wicked. Jeremiah, the prophet, declared that the King of Babylon would overthrow the kingdom of Judah. "The people of Judah will serve their king for 70 years," Jeremiah prophesied.

The king and people of Judah laughed. "Never," they said. "It won't ever happen."

But it did! And when King Nebuchadnezzar besieged Jerusalem, he took captive several young men from leading Jewish families. Daniel was among the group.

Daniel's life was instantly changed. He missed his home, his family and his country. But he took his God with him. Daniel continued to serve God even in his new country.

Daniel was one of the men chosen for special training. King Nebuchadnezzar had ordered that only the best-looking, the strongest and most clever boys should be put into this special school.

"You will be taught by Babylonian teachers," they were told by Ashpenaz, the king's chief. "It will take three years for your schooling. When you are finished, the best of you will get to work for the king himself."

Daniel was determined to do his best, even in this strange country. He studied hard the history, language and culture of Babylon. He even answered to the new name they gave him: Belteshazzar.

God helped Daniel and Daniel learned the secret of being content and flexible in any and every situation. He glorified God anyway. He became wise. Besides all the things he was taught, Daniel could tell people what their dreams meant.

Finally three years had passed. Ashpenaz brought the young men to King Nebuchadnezzar. The king asked the young men difficult questions. Daniel had the wisest answers to them all. Daniel's willingness to adapt to his circumstances gave him a clear mind for his studies. He was chosen by King Nebuchadnezzar to be one of his advisors.

For Discussion

1. Do you like change?
2. Does it upset you when you cannot change the things that happen?

Daniel Puzzle

The children will enjoy fitting the puzzle pieces together and will learn Daniel's secret.

What You Need

- ⇨ puzzle from page 18
- ⇨ crayons
- ⇨ scissors
- ⇨ paper plates
- ⇨ plastic sandwich bags

Before Class

Duplicate the puzzle from page 18 for each child.

What To Do

1. Have the children color and cut out the puzzle.
2. Show how to trace the shapes in their proper positions on a paper plate.
3. Have a race to see who can put their puzzles together first.
4. Give each child a plastic sandwich bag to carry the puzzle pieces.

SAY

Sometimes life may be a puzzle to you. You may wonder, "Why did this happen?" Remember, be flexible and be content. Then you won't find it hard to be happy.

I have learned the secret of being
content in any and every situation.
Philippians 4:12

Daniel's Mailbox

Daniel's Mailbox is a fun craft, and it can be used to review the memory verse.

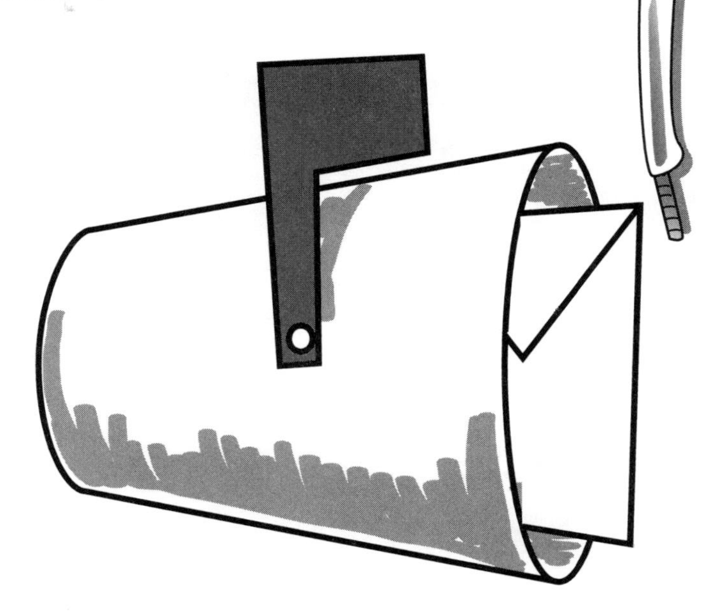

What You Need

- ⇨ mailbox flag, envelope and verse from page 20
- ⇨ large cups
- ⇨ paper fasteners
- ⇨ scissors
- ⇨ glue
- ⇨ red markers or crayons

Before Class

Duplicate the mailbox flag, envelope and verse from page 20. Make a sample craft to use in presenting the memory verse.

What To Do

1. Give each child a mailbox flag to color and cut out.
2. Instruct the children to cut out the envelope and verse.
3. Assist the children in attaching the flag to the cup with a paper fastener.
4. Demonstrate how to fold and glue the envelope.
5. Instruct the children to put the verse in the envelope and place it in the mailbox.

SAY

Daniel had a secret. I think he would be willing to share it with us, so let's read his mail. (Allow the children to read the verse together.) His secret was flexibility. Wherever God led him he could be content.

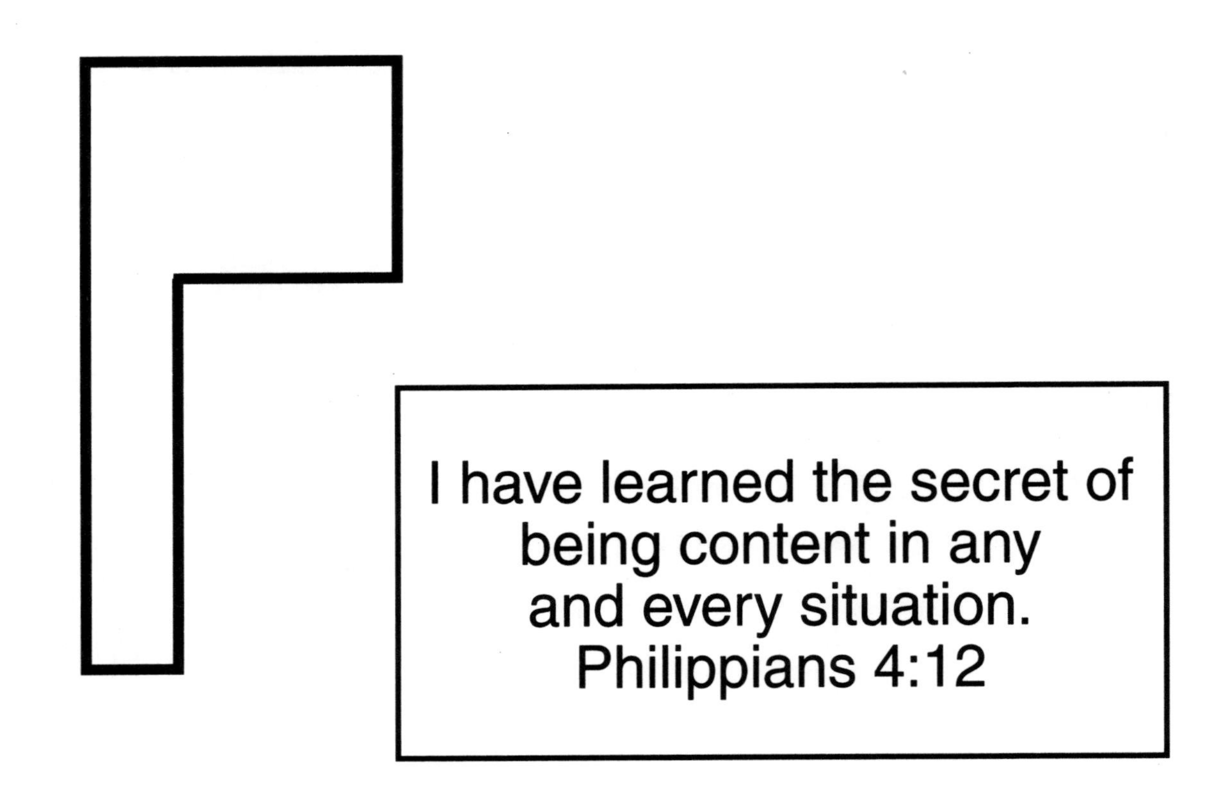
I have learned the secret of
being content in any
and every situation.
Philippians 4:12

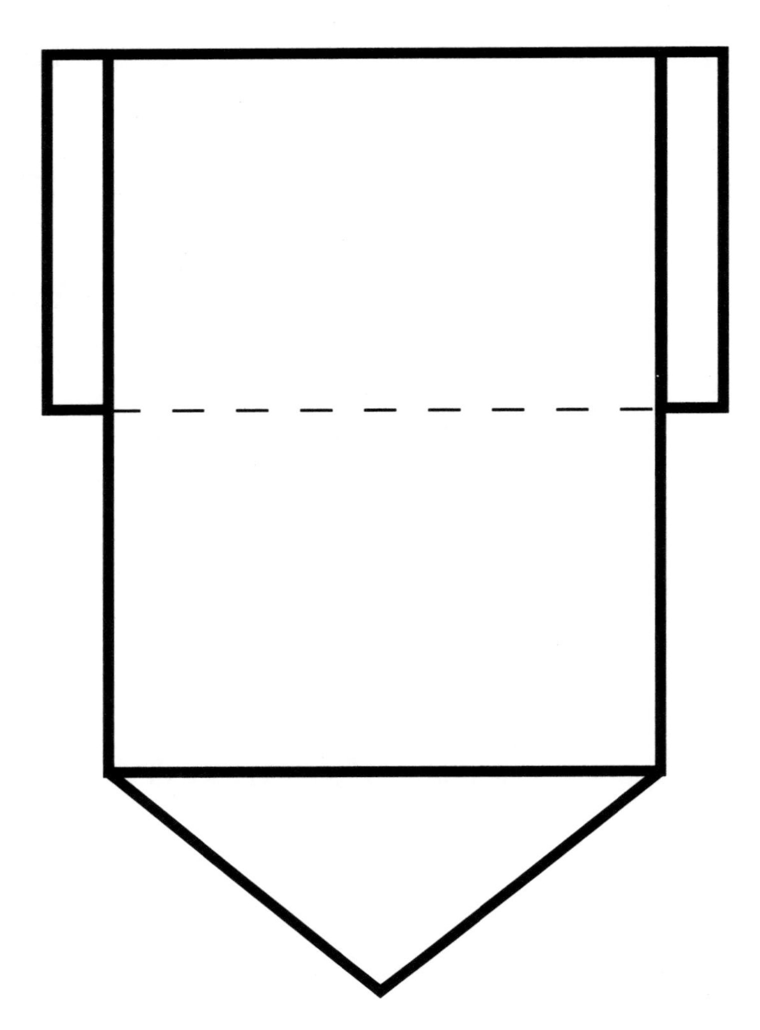

Forgiveness

Memory Verse

Having been justified by his grace, we might become heirs. **~Titus 3:7**

Pig Food

Based on Luke 15:11-19

People surrounded Jesus, waiting to hear the stories He was telling. He told stories of a lost lamb and a lost coin. Then Jesus told about a lost son.

"Once there was a rich farmer who had two sons. One day the younger son came to him. 'I'm not happy living here at home and helping to run this farm,' he said. 'Give me my inheritance now so I can leave.'

"The father gave the son his inheritance. The son was so excited when he left home. He could live like a prince! For a while, the boy enjoyed his new life. He entertained all his friends with rich food, dancing girls and expensive wines. It wasn't long before his money started to dwindle, however, and soon it was all gone. When he was no longer able to entertain his friends, the friends quickly forgot him. His money, not his friendship, was what caused them to hang around him.

"A farmer hired the boy to look after his pigs. One day while working, he looked at the pods from the locust and carob trees that the pigs were eating. He knew they were filled with dark, sweet syrup. He was so hungry he wanted to reach into the pen and get their food to eat.

"How foolish I have been, he thought. *I wasted all my money on parties. I've treated my family in a horrible way, and now I miss them so much. Even the poorest of the men my father hires has good food to eat.*

"The boy made a decision. *I will go back home. I will tell my father how wrong I have been. I'll ask his forgiveness and ask him if I can work as one of the hired men.*

"The boy set out on the long journey home. *I wonder how my father will treat me? Will he allow me to stay home as a servant or will he turn me away?*

"He didn't know how much his father had been missing him. He had often looked down the road, wishing for a glimpse of his son. One day while watching, the father saw a familiar face. His son! Racing down the road as fast as he could, the father reached out and grabbed his son. 'I'm so happy you are home, Son,' he said.

" 'Father,' said the son, 'I have done wrong to you and to God. I'm not worthy to be called your son. Can I please be your servant?'

" 'No,' said his father, 'you are my son. Welcome home! Tonight we will have a party to celebrate your return.' He turned to his servant. 'Bring the best clothes and shoes for my son. Put the family ring on his finger. My son was lost and has come home. Kill the best cow for a steak dinner.' "

Jesus wanted His listeners to see the forgiveness the father had for his son. It was just like the love God has for those who have sinned against Him.

For Discussion

1. Have you ever done something wrong for which you were forgiven?
2. How doing something wrong make you feel?

Pig Food

Creating the snack cup and eating "pig food" will remind your students that God forgives every sin when we ask Him.

What You Need

- ⇨ pattern from page 23
- ⇨ 8 oz. foam cups
- ⇨ wiggle eyes
- ⇨ pink curling ribbon
- ⇨ scissors
- ⇨ glue
- ⇨ tape
- ⇨ cereal

Before Class

Duplicate the pig face from page 23 on pink construction paper for each child. Cut the ribbon in 6" lengths, one per child. You will need two cups per child. For the best "pig food," use your imagination to combine several textures of cereal and include other bite-size edibles like mini marshmallows, gum drops or raisins. Make a sample pig cup so the students can see the finished craft.

What To Do

1. Give each student the duplicated pig head to cut out.
2. Instruct students to lay the pig head on a cup, trace around it and cut it out.
3. Allow the students to glue the pig head to the cup piece. Instruct the students to glue wiggle eyes to the pig's eyes, then glue the head on another cup.
4. Show how to use scissors to curl a 6" length of ribbon.
5. Assist in making a slit in the back of the cup for the pig tail. Give each student a curled tail and assist in poking the end through the cup and taping it on the inside.
6. Allow the students to fill the cup with cereal.

SAY

When you eat the pig food from your snack cup, remember, God wants to forgive your sins, and He will if you ask Him to. Let's pray right now. If you need your sins forgiven, you can repeat the words after me. (Pray slowly, allowing time for students to respond.) Jesus, I believe You are the Son of God. I believe You can forgive my sins. I want to be like the farmer's son and belong to Your family. Please forgive my sins, Jesus. Amen.

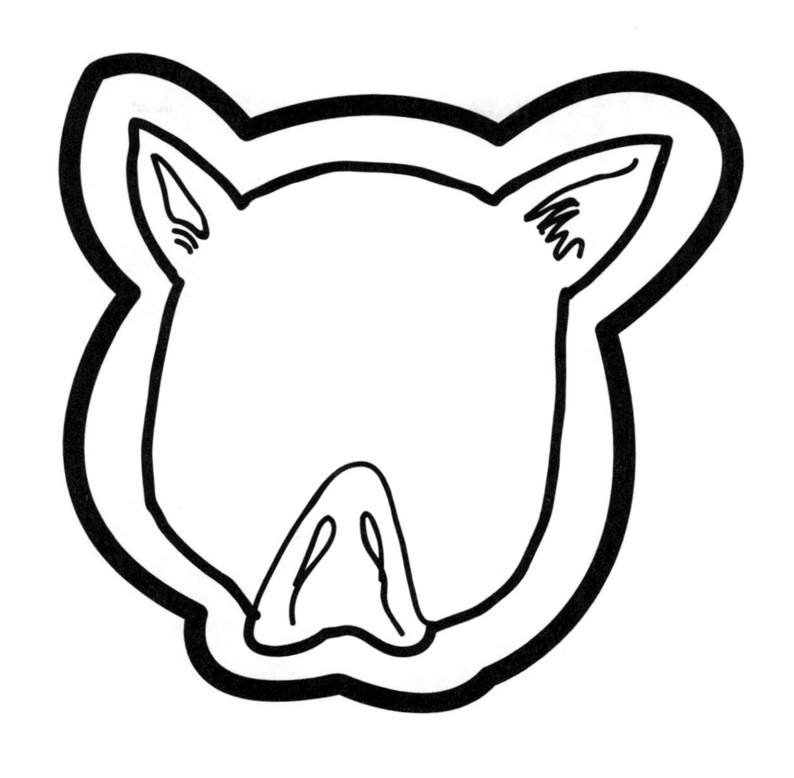

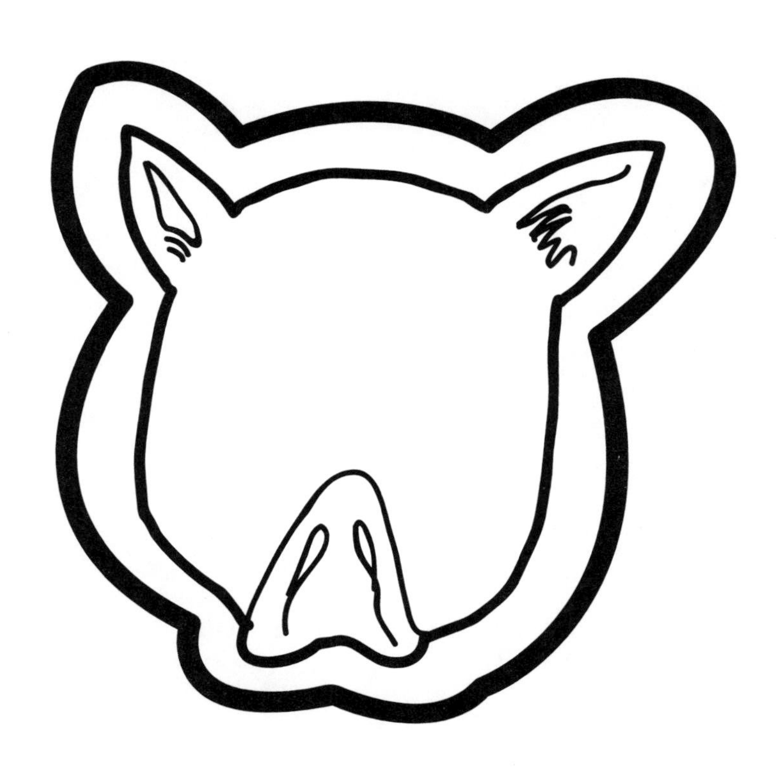

Story Plate

The children will tell the story over and over with this story plate.

What You Need

- ⇨ story pictures from pages 25 and 26
- ⇨ heavy paper plates
- ⇨ felt squares
- ⇨ crayons
- ⇨ scissors
- ⇨ self-stick Velcro strips
- ⇨ glue

Before Class

Duplicate the story pictures from pages 25 and 26 for each child. Cut the Velcro into ¼" strips, nine per child. Make a sample craft to use in telling the story.

What To Do

1. Have the children cut a felt circle to fit a paper plate.
2. Instruct the children to glue the felt to the paper plate. Allow to dry.
3. Give the children the story pictures to color and cut out.
4. Instruct the children to stick a Velcro piece to the back of each story piece.
5. If time permits, allow the children to take turns telling the story with the Story Plate.

SAY

The story of the prodigal son reminds us that no matter how far we are from God, He will welcome us back. Have you wandered from God? Would you like to ask Him to take you back?

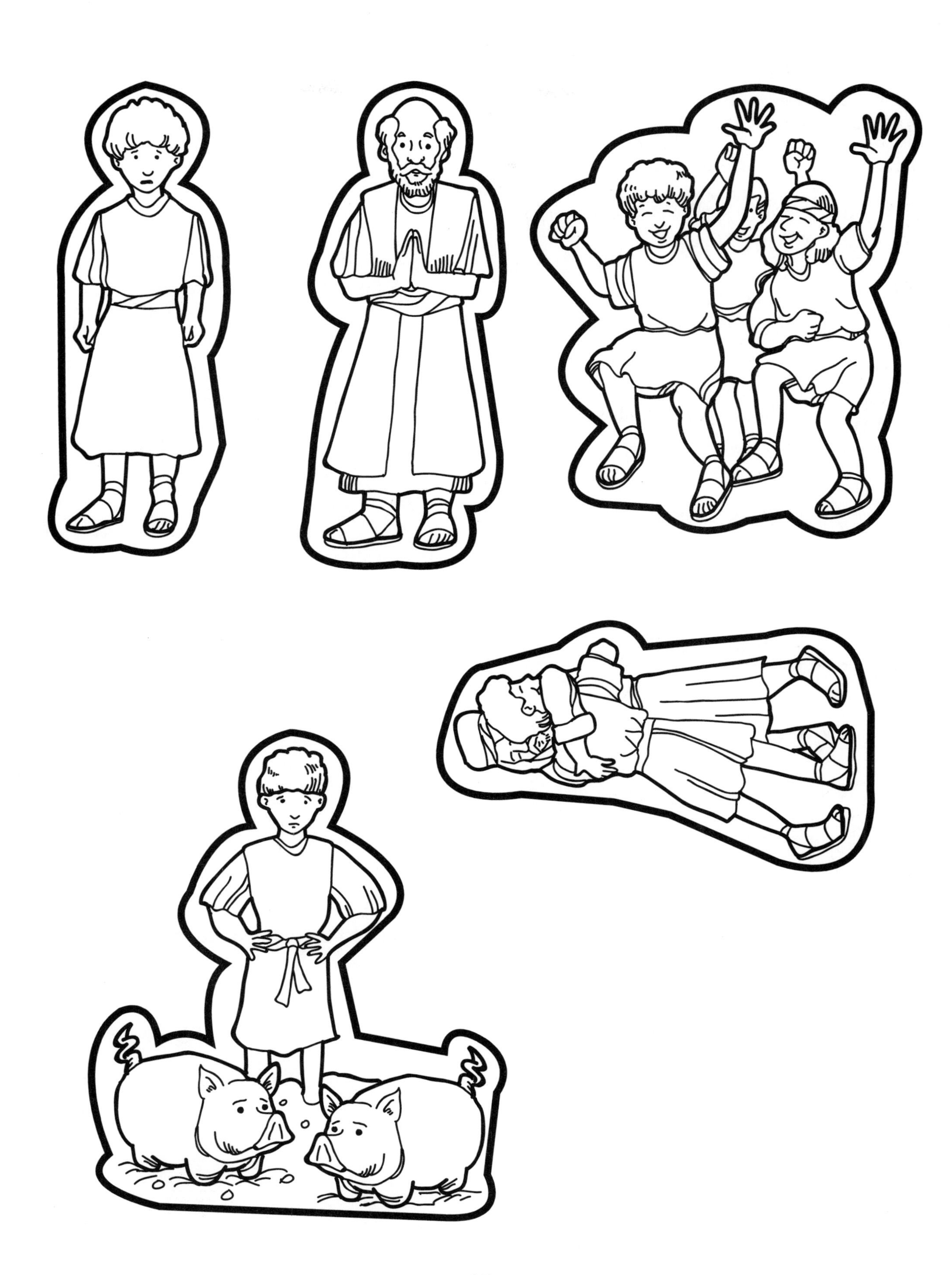

Having
been
justified

by
his
grace

we might
become heirs.

Titus 3:7

Giving

Memory Verse

A generous man will himself be blessed. **~Proverbs 22:9**

A Little Is Most

Based on Mark 12:41-44

In Bible times, part of the temple was called "the treasury." People put their money in the box. They were giving their money to God to thank Him for what He had given to them. We do this today when the offering plate is passed during the church service.

Some religious leaders made poor people feel embarrassed because of the small amount of money they could give. The rich liked to wait until there was a crowd around so everyone could see how much money they gave.

One day a rich man came to the treasury. He waited until there was a crowd. He watched as they put in their money. *Good*, he thought to himself. *I will put mine in after this woman. She is a widow and not likely to have much. That will make my gift seem even larger. Those standing around will never know that I have so much money I won't even miss what I am putting in the box.*

The man chuckled to himself as he stood in line behind the woman. He looked over her shoulder, trying to catch a glimpse of what she was putting in, but she had it wrapped in a bit of cloth. Finally, it was her turn. Carefully she unwrapped her coins. When the rich man saw what was in her hand, his nose lifted a little bit higher in the air. Two coins! Then he saw others shake their heads. He heard the sounds of disgust. "Only two coins, hardly worth more than a penny," he heard someone say.

I have certainly timed this to my best advantage, the rich man thought to himself. Reaching the box, the rich man held up the money and slowly dropped each coin the box.

Then he heard, "Did you see that?" Looking around he saw Jesus and His disciples. The rich man puffed his chest out. Even Jesus saw how much he gave.

Then he heard the next words of Jesus. "The truth is, this poor widow gave more than all these other people today."

"What?" The word was out before the rich man could stop it.

Jesus looked at him. "You gave just a little from what you had left over. You gave what you could easily afford. This widow gave all she had. When she put her coins in the box, she gave all she owned."

For Discussion

1. Do you give to others without worrying about receiving attention or a gift in return?
2. Does giving make you joyful?

A Game of Giving

This giving game will remind your students that God blesses generous giving.

What You Need

⇨ spinner, pointer, game rules and coins from pages 29 and 30

⇨ crayons

⇨ glue

⇨ paper fasteners

⇨ scissors

⇨ paper plates

Before Class

Duplicate the spinner, pointer, game rules and coins from pages 29 and 30 for each child (each student will need 20 coins). Make a sample game so you can demonstrate the game to the children.

What To Do

1. Give each student the duplicated items to cut out.
2. Allow the students to color the game board. Instruct them to color each section a different color.
3. Instruct children to glue the game board to the paper plate front and the rules to the back of the plate.
4. Assist in attaching the pointer to the game board with a paper fastener.
5. Form groups of twos or threes to play the game.

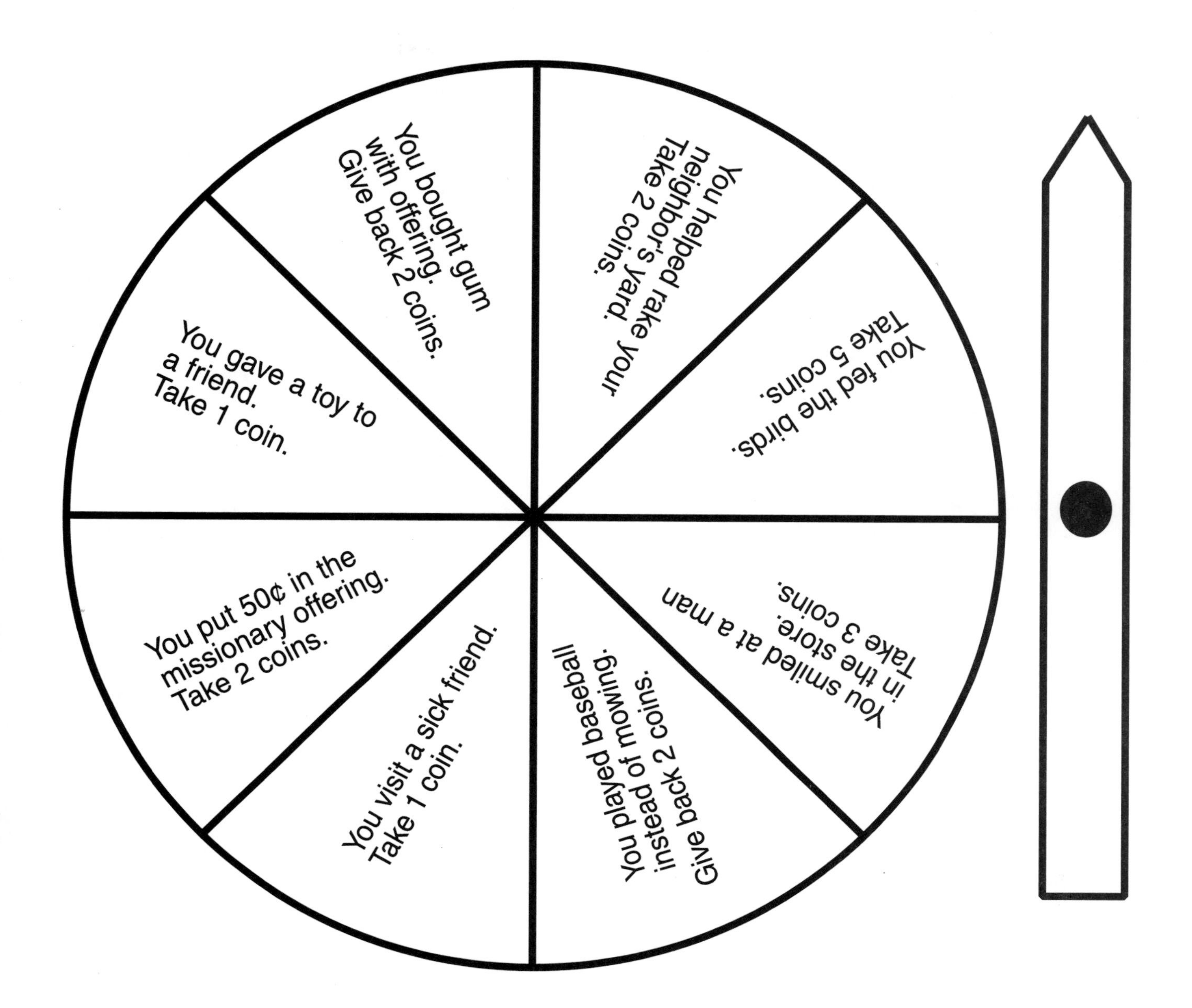

Game Rules

Each player begins with three coins.

The remaining coins are in a pile between the players.

The first player spins and follows directions on the board, then the second player has a turn.

The game is finished when a player reaches 10 coins.

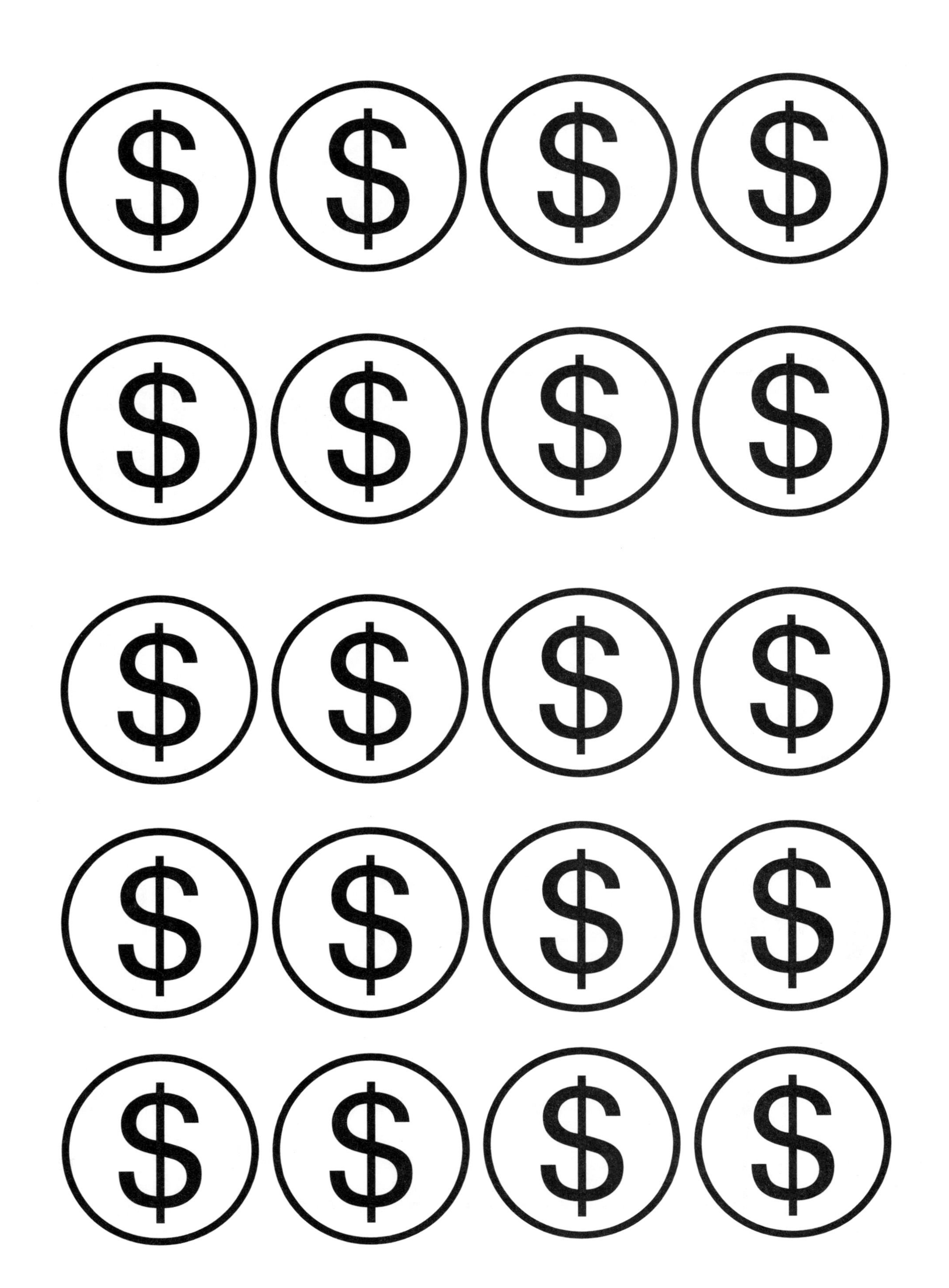

A Giveaway Basket

Your students will enjoy making this basket and they will experience the joy of giving as they choose the recipient of their basket.

What You Need

- basket weave and verse flowers from page 32
- small paper plates
- stapler
- glue
- crayons
- chenille stems
- hole punch
- scissors
- tape

Before Class

Duplicate the basket weave and verse flowers from page 32 for each child. Cut paper plates in half (you will need one full plate and one half plate for each student). Make a sample basket so the children can see the finished craft. You may also join in the discussion of whom you will be giving your basket to.

What To Do

1. Give each child the verse flowers to color and cut out.
2. Instruct the children to staple the half plate to the bottom of the whole plate.
3. Cover the staples with tape to avoid injury.
4. Instruct the children to glue the basket weave pattern to the front of the basket.
5. Assist the children with punching two holes at the top of the basket and attaching a chenille stem for a handle.
6. Allow the children to glue the flowers in the basket so the verse can be read.

SAY

You will find that you will receive a blessing when you give your basket away. Why did the women give all she had to give? Because she knew the secret — it's fun to give!

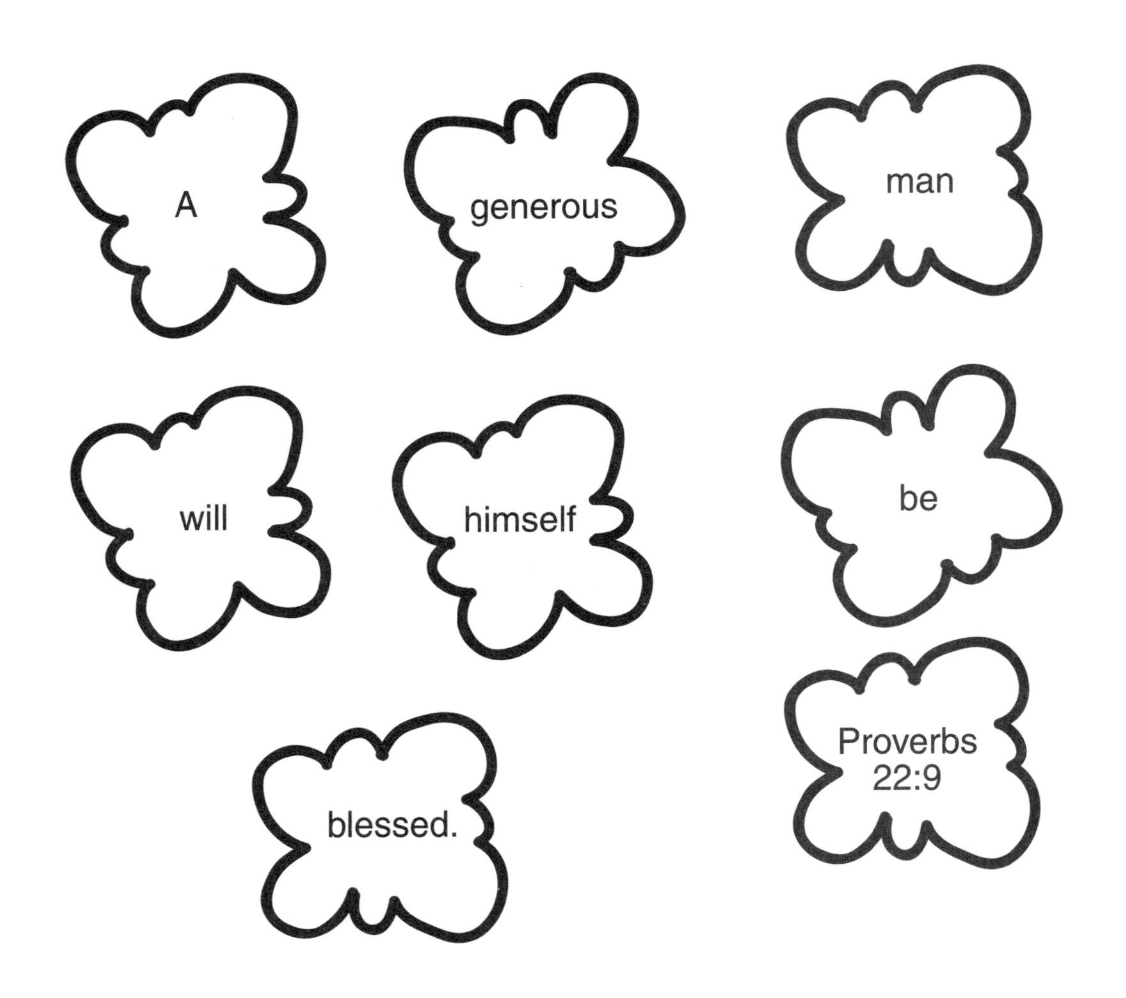
A
generous
man
will
himself
be
blessed.
Proverbs
22:9

God

Memory Verse

The Lord — he is God! ~**1 Kings 18:39**

Who's the True God?

Based on 1 Kings 18:16-40

Elijah was chosen by God to speak God's words. The people were worshipping other gods. King Ahab and his wife, Jezebel, were evil. They had led the people away from worshipping the true God.

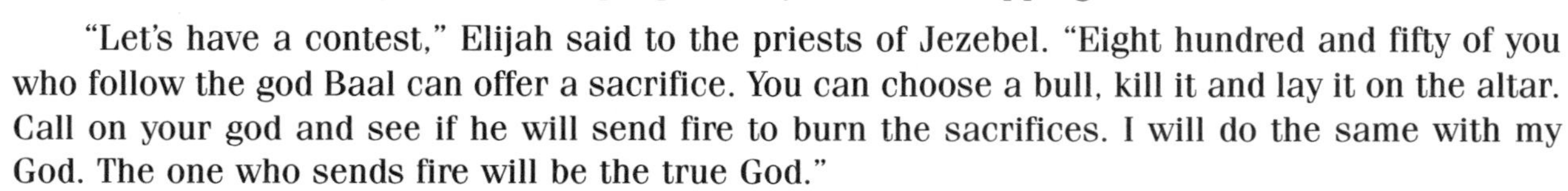

"Let's have a contest," Elijah said to the priests of Jezebel. "Eight hundred and fifty of you who follow the god Baal can offer a sacrifice. You can choose a bull, kill it and lay it on the altar. Call on your god and see if he will send fire to burn the sacrifices. I will do the same with my God. The one who sends fire will be the true God."

The priests took the challenge. They killed the bull and put it on the altar. They prayed and called on their god Baal all morning. "Answer us," they cried. "Oh, Baal, send fire for our altar."

Elijah watched all their praying and smiled. "Louder," he said. "Pray louder, maybe Baal is on a trip, maybe he is having a morning nap."

The priest prayed louder. They pulled their swords out and cut themselves until blood came. They danced, they screamed and they shrieked. Still, Baal did not send fire.

Then Elijah had his turn. He took four large jugs of water and poured them over the altar. He did this three times until the trench he built around the altar was full and the altar was wet.

Elijah lifted his hands toward heaven. Quietly, yet slowly so everyone could hear, Elijah began to pray, "My God, the God of Abraham, Isaac and Israel, show all these here today that You are the true God. I am Your servant, God. You are the true God. Send fire for this sacrifice."

Fire shot out of heaven and struck the earth. The fire ate up the wood, the stones and the bull. Not even the water stopped the fire.

"Elijah's God is the true God!" said the people as they fell on their faces to worship God.

For Discussion

1. What is a false god?
2. Do those gods have power?
3. Whom do you serve?

Elijah's Altar

Your students will enjoy making this altar. It will be a reminder that "The Lord, He is God!"

What You Need

- ⇨ cup wrap and fire on page 35
- ⇨ foam or paper cups
- ⇨ scissors
- ⇨ glue
- ⇨ crayons
- ⇨ small twigs

Before Class

Duplicate the cup wrap and fire on page 35. Make slits in the bottoms of the cups for fire to fit into. Make a sample altar so the children can see the finished craft.

What To Do

1. Give each child a cup wrap and fire to color and cut out.
2. Instruct the children to turn the cups upside-down and glue the wrap to the cup.
3. Allow the children to arrange twigs on the cup and glue them down. (Be sure not to cover up the slit.)
4. Instruct the children to fold the fire on the dashed line and insert it in the slit in the cup.

SAY

King Ahab found out the idol they worshipped had no power. Only God, the true God, is a living God. Who are you serving?

The Lord – he is God!

1 Kings 18:39

Instruments of Praise

Making the Instruments of Praise and singing the song will having your students rejoicing in the true God.

What You Need

- ⇨ song and music notes from page 37
- ⇨ small paper plates
- ⇨ dried beans
- ⇨ stapler
- ⇨ tape
- ⇨ scissors
- ⇨ crayons
- ⇨ glue

Before Class

Duplicate the song and music notes from page 37. Make a sample instrument so the children can see the finished craft and you can play along with the band.

What To Do

1. Give each student a song and music notes to color and cut out.
2. Instruct the children to glue the song to the back of one paper plate and the music notes to the back of the other paper plate.
3. Instruct the children to put 10 beans in one paper plate and top with the other.
4. Assist in stapling the plates together. Cover the staples with tape to avoid injury.
5. Sing the song together to the tune of "Where is Thumbkin?" allowing the children to hit their instruments on the palms of their hands to the rhythm of the music.

SAY

Can an idol love those who worship him? Can he provide for them or protect them? No, but I know who can: the Lord. He is God!

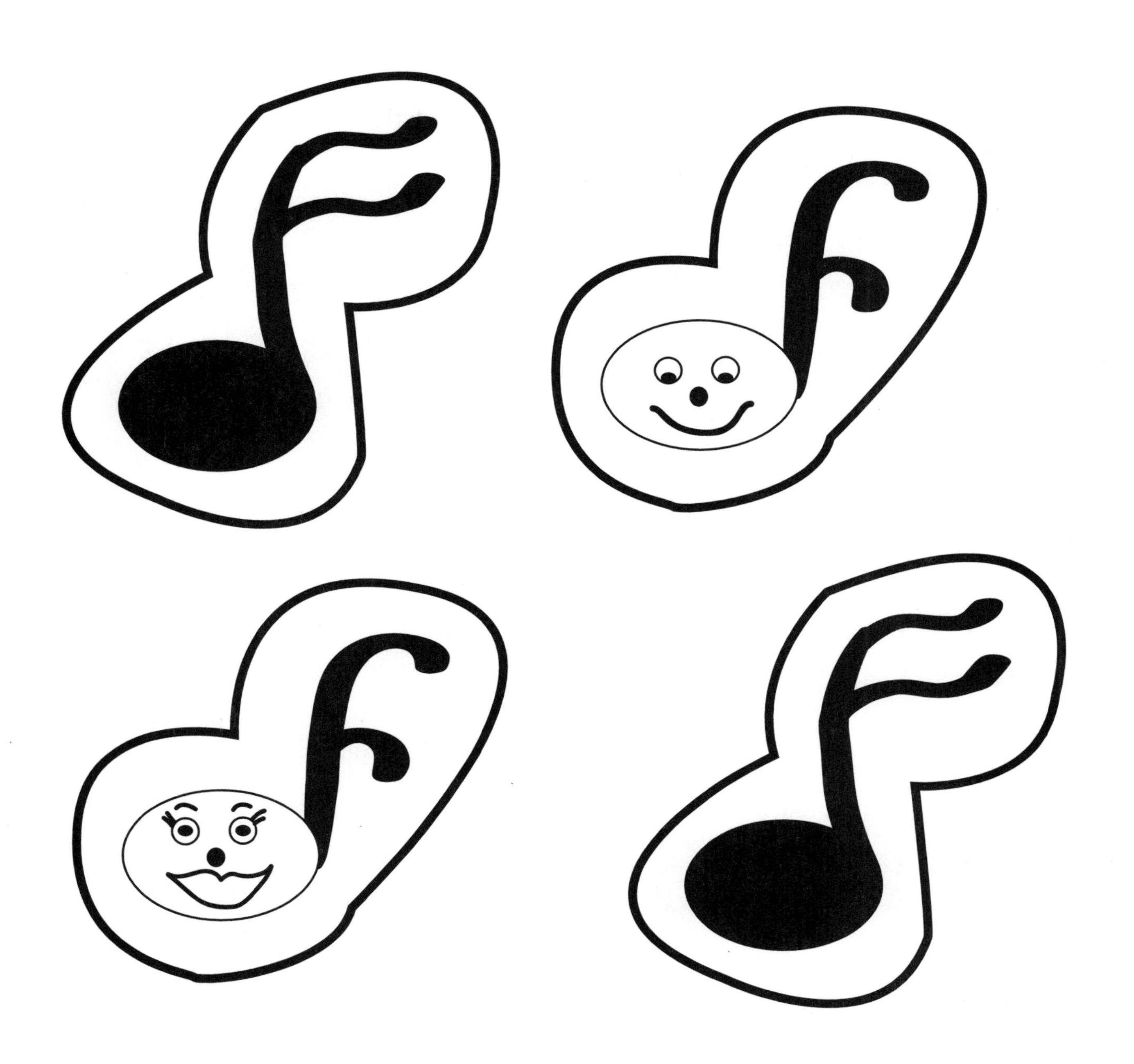

Sing to the tune of "Where Is Thumbkin?"

Who's the true God? Who's the true God?
Do you know? Do you know?
The Lord, He's the true God.
The Lord, He's the true God.
Praise His name! Praise His name!

Helpfulness

Memory Verse

My Father will honor the one who serves me. ~**John 12:26**

A Handsome Victory

Based on Exodus 17:8-13

The Amalekites did not want the Israelites to go into Canaan. This fierce nation had attacked the Israelites. Moses quickly saw that a battle was needed.

"Joshua," said Moses, "I want you to assemble some men together and go into battle tomorrow."

Joshua was stunned. He wasn't trained to be a military commander. While in Egypt he had worked in the slime pits making bricks for Pharaoh's buildings.

But Joshua didn't hesitate for long. He knew Moses was speaking for God. Joshua obediently followed God's commands. He left to choose his men with Moses' promise ringing in his ears: "I will stand on the hill with the rod of God in my hand." He knew Moses would be watching and praying.

The next day, Moses climbed to a nearby hill. Aaron and Hur were with him. They could see the battle begin below. The battle raged all day in the hot sun. Moses held his hands high, silently asking God for victory.

The longer the day went, the more Moses' arms began to ache. But every time Moses would try to rest them, Joshua and his men would begin to lose ground.

Hur and Aaron looked at each other. Their help was needed. With a nod from Aaron, Hur stepped closer to Moses and supported one arm. Aaron, standing on the opposite side, did the same with the other.

A look of peace came over Moses' face. "Thank you, friends," he said before turning back to the battle below.

By the time the sun went down, Joshua and his men had won the victory. As Aaron and Hur removed their support from Moses, his arms dropped heavily to his side. With tears, Moses again thanked his friends. "Thank you for your help. You saw my need before I thought to ask."

Moses built a stone altar to give thanks to God for giving the children of Israel the victory. God told Moses to write down the account of the battle. It was to be a reminder to all who heard that God was powerful. The children of Israel knew that God was their help.

For Discussion

Do you look for opportunities to help those you live with, or do you wait until they ask for help?

Chore Pad

This Chore Pad will encourage your students to ask, "What can I do to help?"

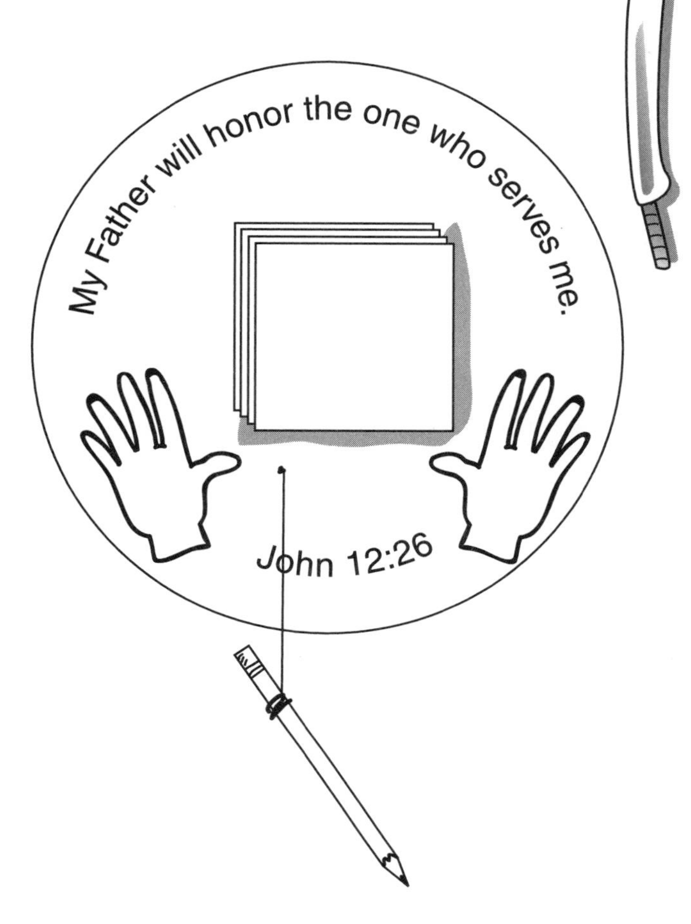

What You Need

- duplicated plate circle from page 40
- 9" paper plates
- 3" square sticky note pads
- stapler
- tape
- yarn
- pencils
- magnet strips
- small stickers
- scissors
- glue
- hole punch

Before Class

Duplicate a plate circle from page 40 on colored paper for each child. Divide the sticky notes into pads of 10 sheets for each child. Make a sample Chore Pad so the students can see the finished craft.

What To Do

1. Allow the children to cut out the plate circle and glue it to a paper plate.
2. Assist the children in stapling the sticky note pad to the plate.
3. Allow the children to decorate the plate with stickers.
4. Assist in punching a hole on the plate and tying yarn through it. Allow the children to tie the other end of yarn to their pencils.
5. Instruct the children to glue a magnet to the back of the plate.

SAY

This Chore Pad will let you know how you can be helpful to others in your family. Place it on the refrigerator. When others need help with a chore they can write it on the pad. Remember, when you choose to be a helpful member of your family, you are pleasing God.

My Father will honor the one who serves me.
John 12:26

Lend a Hand

Using this craft all week will encourage your students to find joy in service.

What You Need

- ⇨ cup wrap from page 42
- ⇨ scissors
- ⇨ glue
- ⇨ crayons
- ⇨ light-colored construction paper
- ⇨ foam cups

Before Class

Duplicate the cup wrap and hand pattern from page 42. Cut out extra hands for the lesson.

What To Do

1. Instruct the students to color and cut out the cup wrap.
2. Instruct the students to trace their hand six times on construction paper and cut them out.
3. Assist in gluing the cup wrap around the cup.
4. After the lesson, instruct the children to write chores they can do on their hands.

SAY

Was it Aaron's and Hur's chore to hold up Moses' hand? No, they did it because they wanted to be helpful. What are some helpful jobs you can do around your home that aren't your assigned chores? (As the children give suggestions, write them on the hands and attach them to a bulletin board.) Write a job on each of your hands and put them in the cup. Each day you can chose an extra job that will be a help to others.

I'll
Lend
a Hand
My Father will honor the one who serves me. ~John 12:26

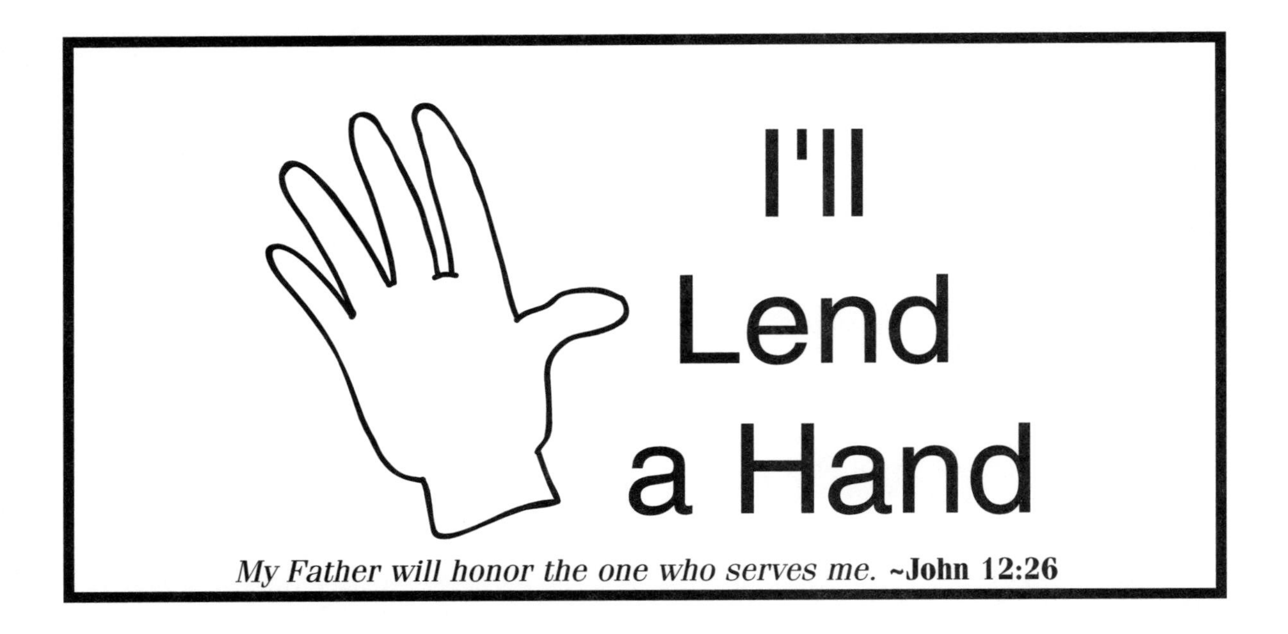
I'll
Lend
a Hand
My Father will honor the one who serves me. ~John 12:26

Confidence

Memory Verse

I can do everything through him who gives me strength. **~Philippians 4:13**

I Spy

Based on Numbers 13:1-14:45

The Israelites were journeying toward Canaan. When they came to the border, they set up camp. Moses was given a command from the Lord. "I brought you out of Egypt and I will bring you into this land of Canaan. Send men to spy out the land, then go in and make it your own."

Moses obeyed God and sent 12 spies into the land. The men spent 40 days looking at the land. Finally they returned.

Two of the spies, Caleb and Joshua, had large pods of grapes with them. The people cheered. The grapes would give them food to eat, either fresh or dried as raisins. They could also be boiled for syrup or pressed for juice.

"There's not only the grapes," said Joshua, his eyes shining. "There are figs and pomegranates that are just as huge."

Caleb nodded, "He's right, it is a land flowing with milk and honey."

"Wait!" said the other spies to the people. "Before you get too excited, listen to the rest."

"Yes," spoke up one spy. "It does have good fruit and the land is fertile, but it is a frightening place."

"That's right," agreed another spy. "The people there are giants. Next to them we were like grasshoppers!"

"Not only are the people giants," said another, "but they live in great walled cities."

Joshua and Caleb looked at them in disgust. "Come on, what are you afraid of? God will be with us."

But the people all shook their heads, "Why didn't we die in the wilderness? Why did God bring us here? Let's go back to Egypt."

God was angry with the people for their insecurity. They couldn't conquer Canaan on their own, but they could with God's help.

"How long will these people anger Me?" asked God. "Why don't they believe that they can do all things with Me? The children of Israel will wander in this wilderness for 40 years because of their insecurity. They shall all die without seeing the promised land — everyone except for Joshua and Caleb who knew that I would help them possess the land."

God's promise was fulfilled. It was Joshua who conquered all the land of Canaan — Joshua and God!

For Discussion

1. How much confidence do you have in yourself?
2. Do you think you can perform hard tasks because you are tough, or because God is helping?

Caleb's Grapes

Creating a pod of grapes with the verse will be a good verse review for your students.

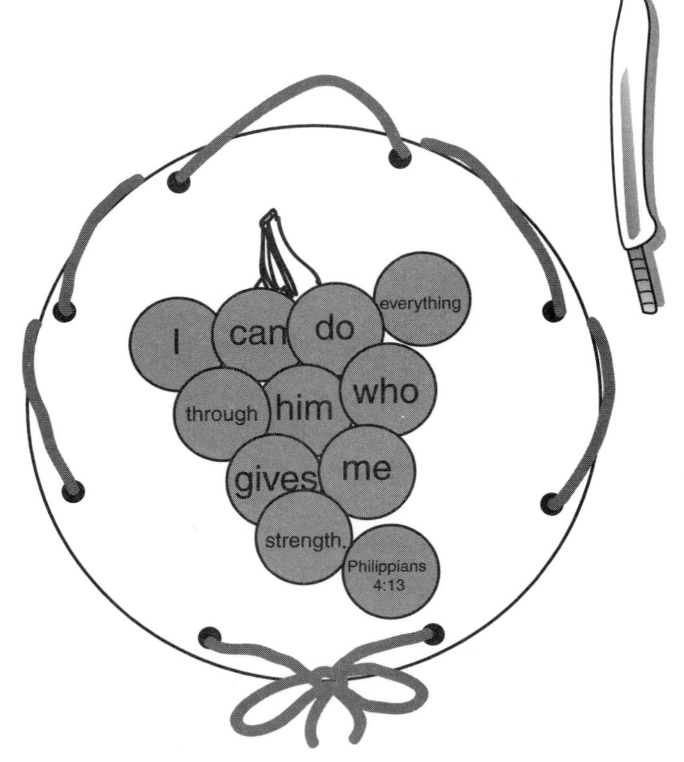

What You Need

- ⇨ grapes from page 45
- ⇨ purple and brown crayons or markers
- ⇨ yarn
- ⇨ hole punch
- ⇨ paper plates
- ⇨ glue
- ⇨ scissors

Before Class

Duplicate the grapes from page 45 for each child. Make a sample craft to use to teach the verse.

What To Do

1. Instruct the children to outline the grapes in purple, then cut them out.
2. Show how to glue the grapes in order so the Scripture may be read.
3. Instruct the children to draw a brown stem and vine on their plate emerging from the bunch of grapes.
4. Allow the students to punch eight holes around the rim of the paper plate.
5. Demonstrate how to thread the yarn through the holes around the plate, leaving long enough ends to tie in a bow at the bottom.

SAY

What do you do when you have to face a difficulty? Do you think, *I can't do this* or do you remember whom to turn to for strength? Like Caleb and Joshua, everyone around you might think you are crazy, but don't limit God…as the verse says, "I can do everything through Him." You can have confidence in God.

I
can
do
everything
through
him
who
gives
me
strength.
Philippians 4:13
I
can
do
everything
through
him
who
gives
me
strength.
Philippians 4:13

I Spy Game

Playing the I Spy Game will help your children to remember that they can face any fearful situation if they have God.

What You Need

- ⇨ verse, game squares, game cards, pie shapes and Joshua from pages 47-49
- ⇨ 9" paper plates
- ⇨ markers
- ⇨ glue
- ⇨ scissors
- ⇨ zipper-type plastic sandwich bags

Before Class

Duplicate the verse, pie shapes, game squares and Joshua from pages 47-49 for each child. Make a sample game so you can play along with the children.

What To Do

1. Have the students divide a paper plate into eight pie pieces with colored markers.
2. Give each child a verse, game square set, game cards and Joshua figure to color and cut out.
3. Allow the children to glue the game pieces in the divided plate. Instruct them to glue the verse on the back.
4. Demonstrate how to fold Joshua on the lines so he stands and glue his head together.
5. Give each child a sandwich bag to store the game pieces.

Game Rules

Turn over (blank side up) the game cards and place them in the middle of the children. No one is to look at anyone else's game board. Together say, "I spy Joshua; where is he?" The children should then place Joshua on one of their pie pieces. Choose one of the cards in the middle to turn over. Everyone who placed Jonah on that pie piece will receive the points the section calls for. Continue until someone has 25 points.

SAY Joshua and Caleb knew what a great God they were serving. They knew that even if there were giants or high walls that God was still bigger. What are you facing? Allow time for student response. Is God bigger than your problem?

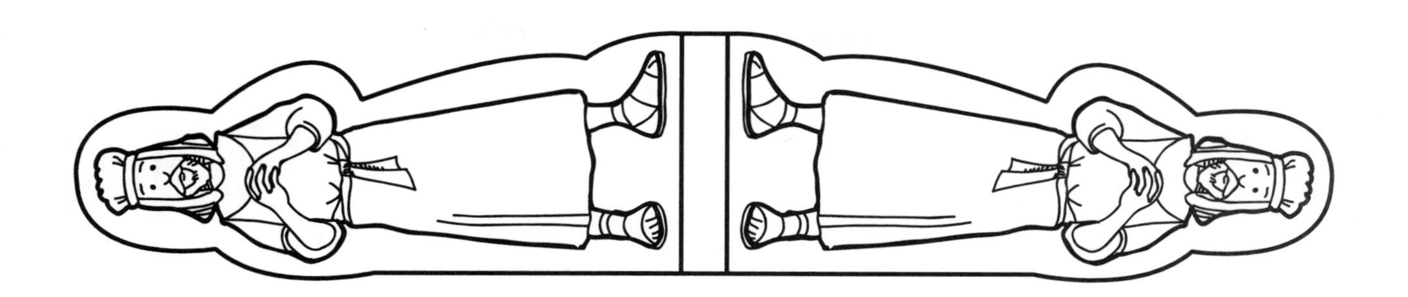

1
2
3
4
5
6
7
8

I can do everything through him who gives me strength.

Philippians 4:13

Mercy

Memory Verse

Blessed are the merciful, for they will be shown mercy. **~Matthew 5:7**

The Miracle Ear

Based on Luke 22:47:51

Jesus knew it was time for Him to be crucified. It would not be easy to endure the suffering He would have to go through. The disciples walked with Him to a garden called Gethsemane. It was a quiet place on the Mount of Olives, a favorite place of them all.

"Stay here a while. I want to pray," Jesus said to His disciples. He took with Him Peter, James and John.

"My heart is full of sorrow. Please watch over Me while I pray," He asked the three disciples.

Jesus knelt on the ground, His face resting on the soil. "Father, I want to obey You. I wish You could take this time of suffering from Me, but if it is Your will I will endure it."

As Jesus knelt He heard the words quietly sink into His soul, "For God so loved the world that He gave His only begotten Son." Jesus nodded in obedience. "Your will be done."

Lifting His head, Jesus heard voices and saw torches light up the darkness. He heard the clanging of armor and swords. Rising from His knees, Jesus shook the sleeping Peter, James and John.

"Come on," He said. "The traitor is coming."

Jesus watched as one of His own disciples came up and betrayed Him with a kiss. That was the signal for the soldiers to seize Jesus. They held Him roughly, not caring that they caused Jesus pain.

Peter grew angry when he saw what they were doing to Jesus. Quickly, he raised his sword and swiped it in the air. One of the soldiers fell to the ground, grabbing his ear.

"Peter," rebuked Jesus. "Put your sword away. I don't need you to protect Me. If I did, I could ask My Father in heaven to send Me 12 armies of angels."

Reaching down to the soldier, Jesus touched him. Immediately the man's ear was healed. John stood and watched Jesus' mercy to the man. He was one of the soldiers who was arresting Jesus.

Why would He show mercy to someone who deserved to die? Peter wondered. The question was answered when He remembered time after time how Jesus taught them to be merciful. He was practicing what He preached.

For Discussion

Have you ever done something you deserved to be punished for but your teacher or your parents showed mercy?

The Soldier's Mask

Your students will be able to understand Jesus' mercy by playacting with this soldier's mask.

What You Need

- ⇨ soldier's face and ears from page 52
- ⇨ paper plates
- ⇨ crayons
- ⇨ scissors
- ⇨ glue
- ⇨ self-stick Velcro
- ⇨ plastic drinking straws
- ⇨ tape

Before Class

Duplicate the soldier's face and ears from page 52. Cut out a solder's face to use as a guide as you cut eye holes in paper plates, one plate per student. Make a sample mask to use in telling the story.

What To Do

1. Give each child a face and ears to color and cut out.
2. Show how to line up the soldier's eyes on the face with the paper plate holes and glue the face in place. Show how to punch out the eyes on the face through the holes.
3. Instruct the children to glue one ear to the soldier.
4. Instruct the children to stick a piece of Velcro on the back of the other ear and a piece on the paper plate where the ear should be.
5. Instruct the children to tape the end of a straw to the back of the paper plate.
6. Read the monologue below and allow the children to pretend they are the soldier Peter attacked.

Monologue: I was just a soldier, doing what I was ordered to do. I didn't know I was helping to arrest the Son of God. They had told me He was a dangerous man. I found out Peter was the dangerous one — he had his sword out in a wink and had cut my ear off before I could blink. Oh, what pain! Then through my agony I heard, "Peter, put your sword away," and I felt tender hands touch my face. The pain stopped as quickly as it had begun. I looked into the eyes of Jesus and saw such love — I knew He was the Son of God.

What do you think it would feel like if your ear was cut off? Did the soldiers deserve to be punished for what they were doing?

Where's The Ear?

Playing this game will be fun for your students and reinforce the memory verse at the same time.

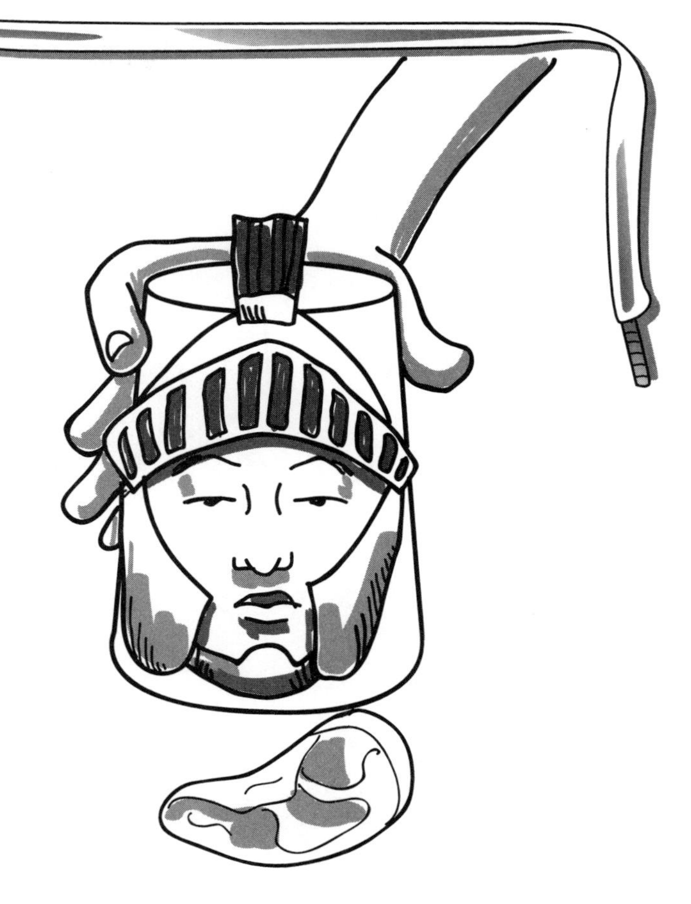

What You Need

- ⇨ soldier and ear from page 54
- ⇨ large foam cups
- ⇨ pencils
- ⇨ crayons
- ⇨ scissors

Before Class

Duplicate the soldier and ear from page 54, three for each child.

What To Do

1. Instruct the students to turn their cups upside down.
2. Have the children color and cut out three soldiers then glue each to a foam cup.
3. Give each student an ear to cut out.
4. Choose a child to hide the paper ear under one of his or her cups, then mix up the cups. Allow the children to guess, one at a time, which soldier cup has the ear underneath it. The first one with the correct guess is next to hide an ear if he or she can repeat the memory verse.

SAY

Let's stand all our soldiers in a row. Jesus faced these men who hated Him but instead of harming them, He had mercy. Is there someone toward whom you need to have mercy?

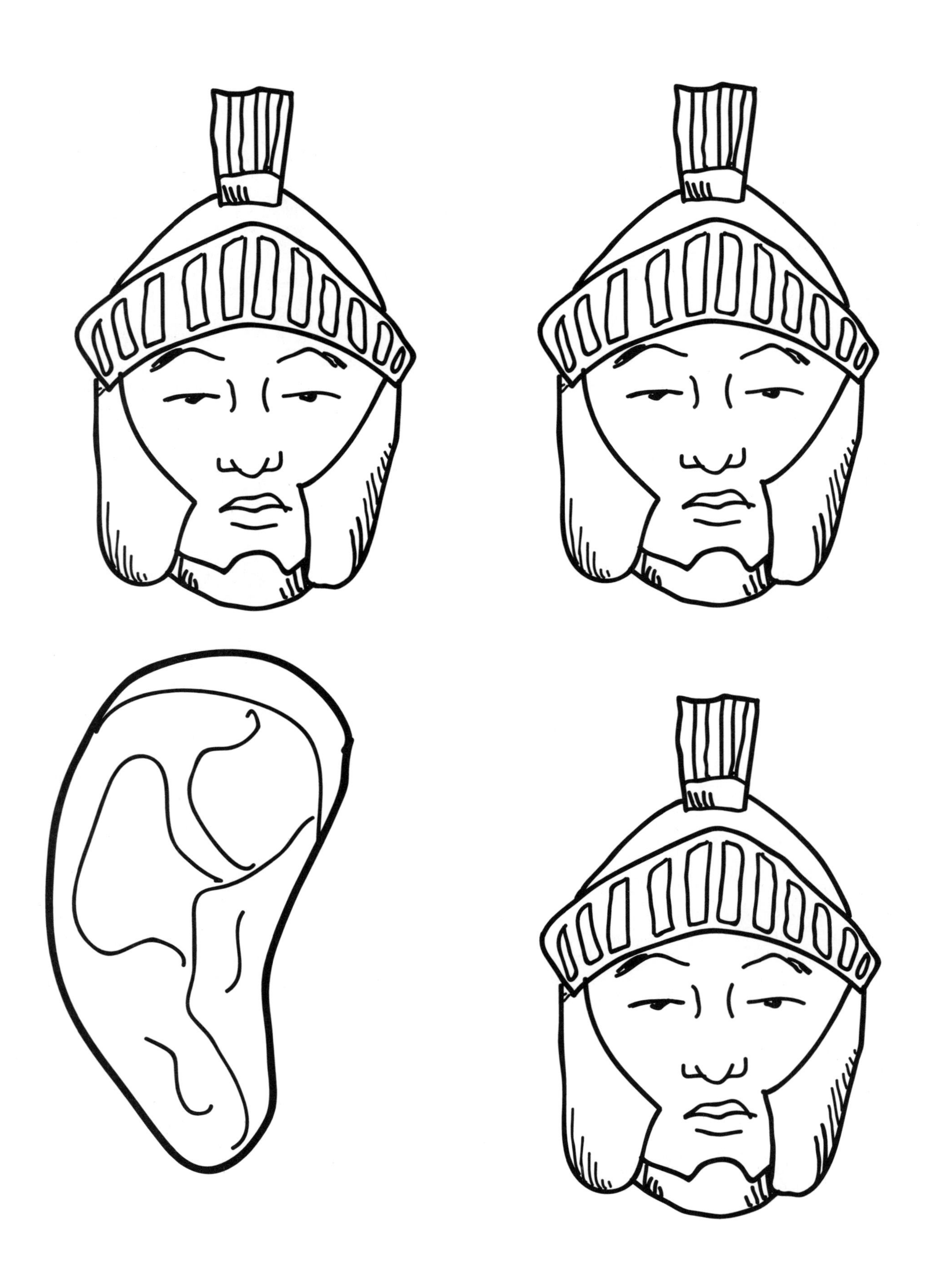

Obedience

Memory Verse

Be obedient in everything.
~2 Corinthians 2:9

A Slimy Motel

Based on Jonah 1-2

Jonah, a prophet who lived in a small village in Galilee, heard the voice of God speaking to him. "Arise, Jonah, go to the great city of Nineveh and preach against their wickedness."

Jonah liked the village where he lived. He was a wise man, both a teacher and a priest to the shepherds and farmers who lived there. Go to Nineveh? He thought to himself. *They are evil people and don't deserve to have a preacher.*

Jonah refused to obey God. Instead of going to Nineveh, he decided to run away to the city of Tarshish. The only way to get there was by sea, so he went to Joppa and found a ship going to Tarshish.

No sooner was the ship out to sea, when a fierce storm arose. The winds blew, whipping the water against the ship. The people and sailors were terrified. "Throw the cargo overboard," they yelled. Everything that could be found was tossed overboard to make the ship's load lighter. Still, the waves threw the ship around like it was a toy.

"Jonah," yelled the captain. "Pray to your God to save the ship."

Jonah knew God would not listen to him because of his disobedience. When the people cast lots to find out who was the cause of the storm, the blame fell on Jonah.

"Yes," he admitted. "I ran away from God. Throw me overboard and the storm will stop."

As soon as they threw Jonah overboard, the wind stopped and the water was calm. As Jonah tried to swim, a large fish swallowed him whole. "Yuck," he said as he looked around at the motel God had prepared for him. "Yuck, it's slimy in here."

"Oh, God," he prayed. "Thank You for keeping me alive. I'm sorry I disobeyed You." For three days and three nights Jonah lived in the slimy motel, praying and begging God to forgive his disobedience. Then the fish vomited Jonah onto dry land.

This time, Jonah obediently went to Nineveh. "You are wicked!" he preached to the people there. "God is going to destroy your city."

The people of Nineveh were afraid and sorry for their evil ways. Even the king was sorry. They begged God to forgive them, promising to give up their wicked ways. God heard them and decided not to destroy the city.

Jonah had obeyed God, but he didn't want to. Now God was going to save the people he resented. Jonah built a shelter outside the city walls where he sat and pouted. God made a vine grow up that shaded Jonah from the sun. The next morning, a worm ate the roots of the vine so that it withered and died. Jonah was hot and miserable. "I wish I were dead," he said.

"Why are you angry?" asked God. "You neither planted nor watered the vine. And why do you resent the love I have for the people of Nineveh? There are thousands of people that will be saved."

Jonah repented of his resentful obedience.

For Discussion

1. Is it easy to be obedient?
2. Do you willingly do chores you don't want to do or do you grumble?

Jonah Nesting Cups

Your students will have fun with these nesting cups. Playing with them will remind them that obedience pays!

What You Need

- ⇨ pictures and poem from page 57
- ⇨ cups (four different sizes)
- ⇨ glue
- ⇨ crayons
- ⇨ scissors

Before Class

Duplicate the pictures of Jonah and poem from page 57 for each child. Make a set of nesting cups so the children can see the finished product.

What To Do

1. Give each child the pictures and poem to color and cut out.
2. Instruct the children to glue the pictures as follows (largest to smallest):

   1st (largest) cup: water and boat

   2nd cup: fish swallowing Jonah

   3rd cup: Jonah praying

   4th (smallest) cup: Jonah free
3. Demonstrate how to stack the cups.
4. Say the poem together, uncovering each picture as you say the corresponding line.

Down in the water
poor Jonah was thrown.
Along came a fish and
swallowed him down.
Jonah prayed and asked forgiveness
in that dark, creepy belly.
The fish burped him up;
he was thankful and smelly!

Poor Jonah Game

As the students play the Poor Jonah Game they will be reminded to be obedient.

What You Need

⇨ Jonah and fish from page 59

⇨ large foam cups

⇨ hole punch

⇨ crayons

⇨ glue

⇨ yarn

Before Class

Duplicate the fish and Jonah from page 59 on heavy paper. Cut an 18" length of yarn for each student. Make a sample game so the children can see the finished project.

What To Do

1. Give each student the duplicated Jonah and fish to color and cut out.
2. Show where to fold Jonah and glue it together.
3. Instruct the children to glue the fish to the cup.
4. Assist in punching a hole in the rim of the cup and a hole in Jonah where indicated.
5. Assist in tying the yarn to the holes. To play the game, the students should swing the cup and try to land Jonah in the whale (the cup).

SAY

It took a large fish to teach Jonah obedience. Let's say the memory verse together and see if we can get Jonah in his slimy motel before we finish the verse.

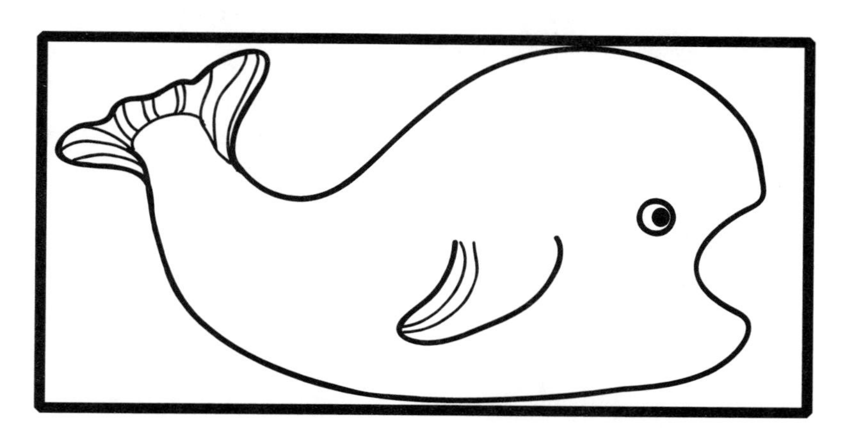

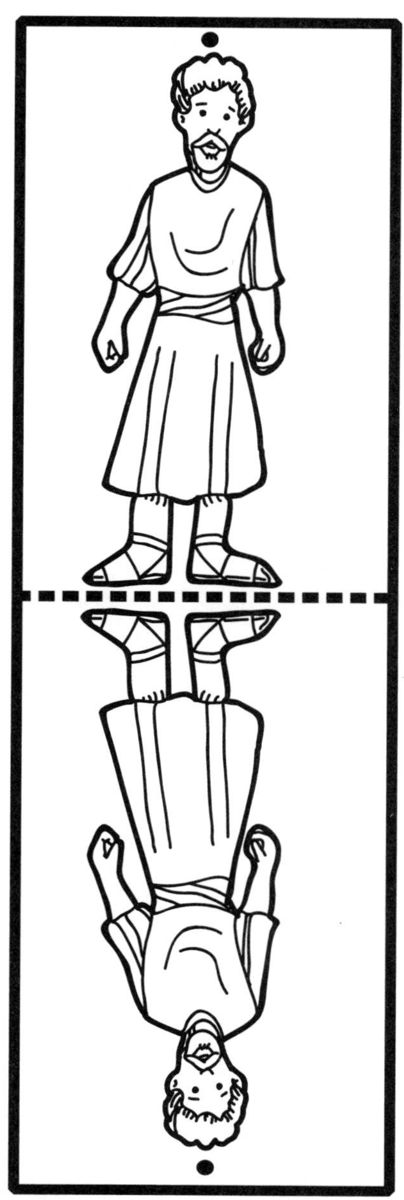

Providence

Memory Verse

My God will meet all your needs.

~Philippians 4:19

Fed by the Birds

Based on 1 Kings 17:1-6

The king was angry with Elijah. He came before the king with a message from God: "The children of Israel have turned against God and do wicked things. There will not be any dew or rain until I say so." By the time King Ahab understood what Elijah said, Elijah had disappeared.

"Where's Elijah?" he demanded of the servants in his palace. They could not find him. "Where's Elijah?" he demanded publicly.

"We don't know," he was told over and over. "The Lord takes him here and there like the wind."

The king's wife, Jezebel, was angry, too. She worshipped the god of Baal. "He's the god of the rain," she said. "How dare he say it wouldn't rain until he said so."

Still, no one could find Elijah. God had hidden him in a cave by a brook, east of Jordan. People searched everywhere, but they could not find him.

Every morning the ravens came to Elijah. They carried bread and meat in their beaks. Elijah enjoyed his morning meal. He drank water from the brook with it.

In the evening, when Elijah's stomach started to rumble, he watched the sky for a sign of the dark birds. They flew near again, bringing more meat and bread. Elijah enjoyed his evening meals, watching the sun disappear and the stars begin to twinkle in the sky.

"Thank You, God," he prayed each day. "Thank You for taking care of me. You gave me this brook for water to drink. You send ravens with my food. How good You are to me!"

For Discussion

1. Does God give you everything you want? A new bike? A computer game?
2. Does He give you the things you need? What are they?
3. What is the difference between a want and a need?

Delivery Birds

Your students will enjoy making this message bird, and as it twirls around it will be a reminder of God's providence.

What You Need

- ⇨ verse, beak and wings from page 62
- ⇨ paper plates
- ⇨ string
- ⇨ tape
- ⇨ scissors
- ⇨ chenille stems
- ⇨ glue
- ⇨ wiggle eyes

Before Class

Duplicate the verse, beak and wings from page 62 for each child. Cut the chenille stems into four pieces per child. Cut one 8" length of thread per child. Make a sample bird to hang in your classroom doorway or window.

What To Do

1. Have the students fold a paper plate in half and trace and cut out a half heart on the fold.
2. Allow the children to cut out the wings, beak and verse.
3. Instruct the children to color the beak and wings, then glue them in place.
4. Demonstrate how to fan four chenille stem pieces to make a tail. Tape these in place on the bird.
5. Instruct the children to glue the bird body together.
6. Allow the children to glue the verse to the bird's beak.
7. Show how to loop thread and tape it to the back of the bird for a hanger.

SAY

Our verse says, "My God will meet all your needs." What are some needs you have? (food, clothes, place to sleep) How has God met those needs? Does that help you believe God will supply other needs you have?

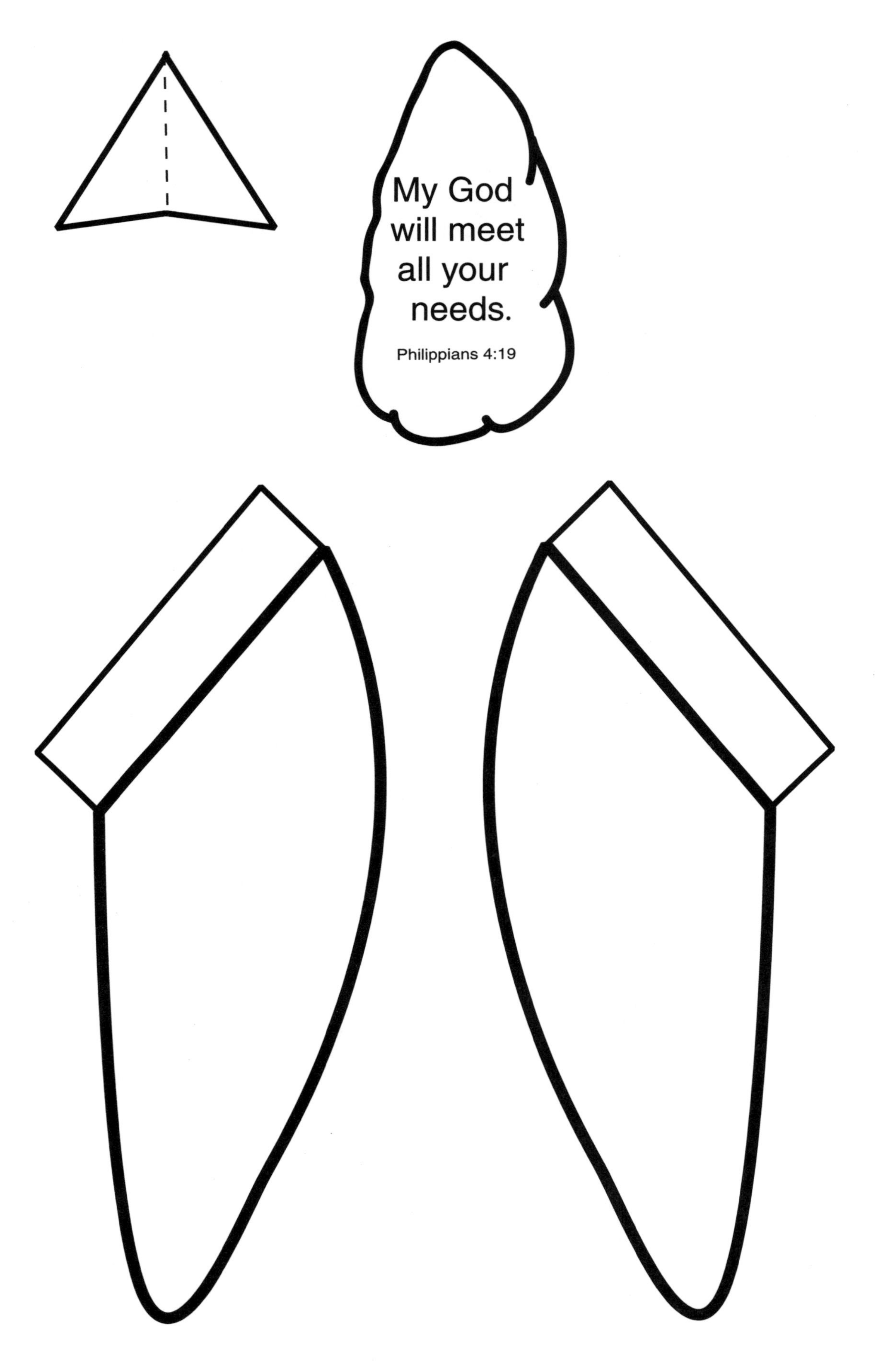
My God will meet all your needs.
Philippians 4:19

Flying Bird

The students will have fun seeing whose bird will fly the fastest to get the food to Elijah.

What You Need

⇨ bird circle from page 64

⇨ paper plates

⇨ glue

⇨ crayons

⇨ scissors

Before Class

Duplicate the bird circle on page 64 for each child. Make a sample craft to demonstrate what the children will be making.

What To Do

1. Allow the children to color the bird circle and cut it out.
2. Instruct the children to glue the circle to a paper plate.
3. See whose bird will "fly" the farthest (throw it like a Frisbee™).

SAY

What would you think if a bird brought your supper to you? God didn't supply Elijah's needs like we would have, but his needs were supplied. God always gives us what we need.

My God will meet your needs.
Philippians 4:19

Reliability

Memory Verse

Always give yourselves fully to the work of the Lord. ~**1 Corinthians 15:58**

The King's Right-Hand Man

Based on Genesis 41:37-45

Pharaoh sat up in bed, trembling and frightened. *What a dream!* he said to himself. *I wish I knew what it meant.*

Pharaoh reviewed the dream in his mind. It seemed as though he was standing on the bank of the Nile. Seven fat cows came up and fed in the meadow. Then, up came seven other cows who were thin and ugly. The thin cows ate the fat cows. Whatever could it mean?

All the wise men of Egypt couldn't tell the king what his dream meant. But God showed Joseph the meaning of the dream and he interpreted it for the king.

"God is showing you what is going to happen, Pharaoh," Joseph said. "The fat cows stand for seven years in which there will be plenty to eat and drink. But after those seven years, the crops will not grow. That is represented by the seven thin cows. The famine will last seven years and many will be hungry."

Pharaoh put his head down. "What will happen to us? What will we do?" he asked.

"You should place someone in charge of all of the food," Joseph suggested. "Store the leftover food. Then when the crops won't grow, the people can eat what we already have stored away."

Pharaoh nodded his head. "I will want someone I can rely on, one whom I can trust to do the work and do it well. Joseph, your God is always with you. You are someone I can rely on. You will be in charge of all food storage. No one will be greater than you, except for me."

Joseph was surprised, but he was determined to be someone Pharaoh could rely on. He knew God would help him. Joseph was only 30 years old, but he worked hard storing up all the food from the seven good years. When the famine finally came, he opened up the storehouses. There was plenty for everyone.

For Discussion

1. How many times does you mother have to ask you to take out the trash (wash the dishes, clean up your room, etc.)?

2. Can you be counted on to do what is asked of you, without being reminded?

Here I Am Cup

This craft is a fun way for children to learn to be reliable.

What You Need

- ⇨ Joseph figure and verse from page 67
- ⇨ small foam cups
- ⇨ plastic drinking straws
- ⇨ stapler
- ⇨ scissors
- ⇨ glue
- ⇨ crayons
- ⇨ tape

Before Class

Duplicate the Joseph figure and verse from page 67 for each child. Make a sample craft so the students can see the finished project.

What To Do

1. Give each child a Joseph figure and verse to color and cut out.
2. Assist the children in folding the Joseph figure over the straw and stapling it in place. Cover the staple with tape to prevent injury.
3. Have the students glue the verse to the outside of the cup.
4. Help the students cut a slit in the bottom of the cup that the straw can fit through.
5. Instruct the children to put the straw end down the hole until Joseph cannot be seen.
6. Show how to pop up Joseph.

SAY

Joseph was the king's right-hand man because he was willing and ready to do whatever was asked of him. You can be God's worker, too, if you are ready and willing to obey.

Always give yourselves
fully to the work
of the Lord.
1 Corinthians 15:58

Always give yourselves
fully to the work
of the Lord.
1 Corinthians 15:58

Mr. Reliability

The children will enjoy making Mr. Reliability. By taking the pledge, the children will remember to be reliable.

What You Need

- ⇨ face features from page 69
- ⇨ crayons
- ⇨ scissors
- ⇨ glue
- ⇨ paper plates
- ⇨ balloons

Before Class

Duplicate the face features from page 69 for each child. Make a sample helper so the children can see the finished craft.

What To Do

1. Give each child the face features to color and cut out.
2. Assist the children as they cut an X in the middle of a paper plate.
3. Instruct the children to write, "I, (child's name) pledge to be a reliable helper" along the edge of the plate.
4. Give each child a balloon to inflate.
5. Instruct the children to glue the face features in place on the balloon.
6. Show how to pull the knot in the balloon through the X.
7. Read the pledge below to the class and invite those who wish to take the pledge with you to do so.

Pledge

I pledge to be a reliable helper.
I will always give myself to the work of God.

SAY

Have you ever asked someone to help you and he or she said, "Not now" or "Later" or "I can't?" How does that make you feel? (Allow time for students to respond.) Be reliable and ready to help when asked.

Respect

Memory Verse

In humility consider others better than yourselves. **~Philippians 2:3**

A Pouting King

Based on 1 Kings 21:1-29

In the midst of the beautiful valley of Jezreel stood the palace of King Ahab. Wherever he looked, King Ahab could see beautiful vineyards. The closest and most beautiful vineyard was so close to Ahab's palace that it seemed to be a continuation of his palace.

King Ahab looked at the vineyard, saw the deep purple of the grape clusters, and wished the vineyard belonged to him. *Maybe Naboth will sell me his vineyard,* he thought. *I'll give him a good price for it.*

But when Naboth heard of the king's offer he said, "This land has been in my family since the days of Joseph. I have lived here all my life. The Lord forbids a man to give up his father's inheritance."

Ahab knew this was the law, but he wasn't used to having anyone say no to him. He was angry, and as the afternoon hours passed he started to pout. When supper time came he refused to eat. He just turned his head to the wall and pouted.

"Come on, Ahab," begged his wife, Jezebel. "What's wrong?"

"Naboth won't sell me his vineyard."

Not once did King Ahab and his wife think to respect Naboth and his decision. "Aren't you the king?" Jezebel asked. She laughed and said, "Don't worry anymore about this. I'll take care of it."

Jezebel wrote letters to the elders and nobles of the city. "Proclaim a fast and place Naboth in a position of great importance. Have men accuse him of speaking against God." Jezebel knew they could stone him for this crime. She signed the letters with Ahab's name and sealed them with the royal seal.

The wicked deed was carried out just as planned. When Jezebel heard of it she laughed with the King. "The vineyard is yours now, Ahab," she said.

Ahab was eager to walk in his new vineyard. As he was inspecting the vines of grapes, a man suddenly blocked his way. It was the prophet, Elijah.

"You cruel man! Have you no respect? This vineyard has been bought with the blood of an innocent man. The dogs will lick your blood from the roadside just as they have Naboth's. Jezebel's death will be just as cruel and violent as yours."

Ahab's eyes were opened and he saw the evil thing he had done. He tore his clothes and put on sackcloth. He refused to eat.

Elijah visited the king again. "God said He would be merciful to you because you have seen your great sin. You can live out your life in peace, but disaster will come to your sons' lives."

For Discussion

Have you ever looked at a classmate and thought, *I am better than him (or her); the teacher should give me more privileges?*

Tell-Tell Mirror

The children will enjoy hanging this mirror in their room. It will be a constant reminder to keep their attitudes in check.

What You Need

- ⇨ verse, hearts and baseballs from page 72
- ⇨ crayons or markers
- ⇨ scissors
- ⇨ glue
- ⇨ paper plates
- ⇨ aluminum foil
- ⇨ yarn
- ⇨ tape

Before Class

Duplicate verse, hearts and baseballs from page 72. Cut the yarn into 3" lengths. Make a sample mirror so the children can see the finished craft.

What To Do

1. Give each child a verse and allow them to choose between hearts or baseballs.
2. Instruct them to color and cut out the pieces.
3. Have the students cut the center from a paper plate.
4. Show how to glue a piece of foil to the back of the paper plate rim.
5. Show where to glue the verse and hearts or baseballs around the rim.
6. Demonstrate how to make a loop with the yarn and tape it to the back of the mirror rim.

SAY

What kind of face would King Ahab have seen if he would have looked in a mirror? (Allow time for students' response.) Everyone make a pouting face. Look around you. Does it make you feel good when you see someone pouting? Now let's all smile and think about the One who sees us when we're pouting. Let's keep our happy faces on!

In humility consider others better than yourselves.

Philippians 2:3

Upside Down Frown

The children can take the pouting king home to remind them that all they need to do to change their attitude is turn their frowns upside down.

What You Need

- ⇨ king face, frown and verse from page 74
- ⇨ foam cups
- ⇨ scissors
- ⇨ crayons
- ⇨ glue
- ⇨ paper fasteners

Before Class

Duplicate the king face, mouth and verse from page 74. Make a sample king so the children can see the finished craft.

What To Do

1. Give each child a face, mouth and verse to color and cut out.
2. Instruct the children to glue the king face to one side of the cup and the verse to the other side.
3. Assist in attaching the frown with a paper fastener.

SAY

Look how miserable King Ahab looks! Turn his frown upside down and see if he looks better. Remember, when you are tempted to pout, make a quick attitude change by turning that frown upside down.

In humility
consider others
better than
yourselves.

Philippians 2:3

Second Coming

Memory Verse

Keep watch, for you do not know on what day your Lord will come.

~Matthew 24:42

What Time Will He Come?

Based on Matthew 25:1-13

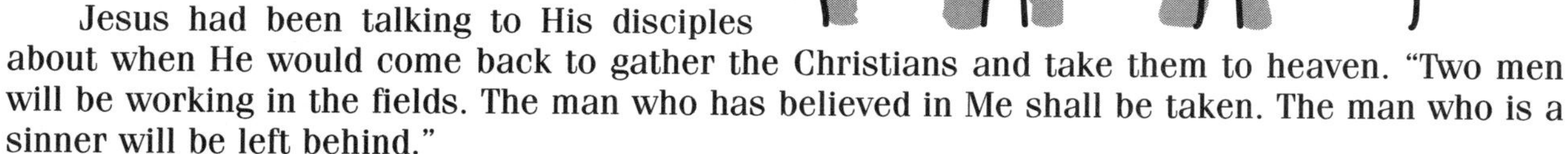

Jesus had been talking to His disciples about when He would come back to gather the Christians and take them to heaven. "Two men will be working in the fields. The man who has believed in Me shall be taken. The man who is a sinner will be left behind."

The disciples looked at each other. Not one of them wanted to be left behind! They were so thankful they believed Jesus was the Son of God.

Jesus went on, "Two women will be preparing food. The one who has believed in Me will be taken and the other left behind."

"When, Lord?" asked Peter. "What day will You come back?"

"You do not know, Peter," answered Jesus. "No one will know when I am going to return. You must just be ready."

Jesus told them a story to explain what it meant.

"There were ten young women who were waiting for the bridegroom. They didn't know when he would be coming, but the wedding celebration couldn't begin without him.

"These young women were carrying lamps. Five of them were wise, remembering that the oil in their lamps would only last about three hours. They knew they might have to wait longer than that before the bridegroom came, so they carried a jar of extra oil with them in case their lamps went out. The other five foolishly did not.

"The wait was long, and one by one each of the women fell asleep. Soon it was midnight and they awakened hearing, 'The bridegroom is coming. Come and meet the bridegroom!' The women sat up and reached for the lamps. The five foolish women found their lamps had gone out.

" 'Please,' they begged, 'give us some of your oil.' But the five who had extra oil knew they didn't have enough for their lamps and the lamps of the others. 'No,' they said. 'Go and buy some for yourselves.'

"While the foolish girls were gone, the bridegroom came. The five young women were waiting with their lamps burning brightly. The bridegroom took them with him to the wedding celebration, shutting and bolting the door behind them.

"The foolish women bought their oil and came as quickly as they could. They tried to get in but found the door locked. They beat with their fists on the door calling, 'Lord, Lord, please let us in.'

"But the bridegroom answered from behind the closed door, 'I don't know who you were. You were not waiting when I came.' "

Jesus stopped and looked at His disciples. "The message of this story is to be prepared. You do not know when I will return."

For Discussion

1. When do you think Jesus will come back to earth? When you are 12? A teenager? When you are in college?
2. Do you know when Jesus will return?

Coming in the Clouds

Making this craft will reinforce to your students the lesson of the return of Jesus.

What You Need

⇨ figure of Jesus and verse blocks on page 77

⇨ 9" paper plates

⇨ scissors

⇨ yarn

⇨ hole punch

⇨ glue

⇨ cotton balls

⇨ crayons

Before Class

Duplicate the figure of Jesus on page 77. Make a sample craft to use as an example.

What To Do

1. Give each child a figure of Jesus and verse blocks to color and cut out.
2. Have them cut out the middle of the paper plates, leaving only the rim.
3. Assist the children in punching two holes in the plate and one in the figure of Jesus.
4. Assist in tying the figure of Jesus to the paper plate and a yarn hanger at the top.
5. Instruct the children to pull the cotton balls apart and glue them to the top of the plate.
6. Allow the children to glue the verse blocks in order on the plate, starting on the left side and circling to the right side.

SAY

Do you think Jesus will come tomorrow? Who knows? No one knows. Jesus could come back before our class is finished. Are you ready for Him to come?

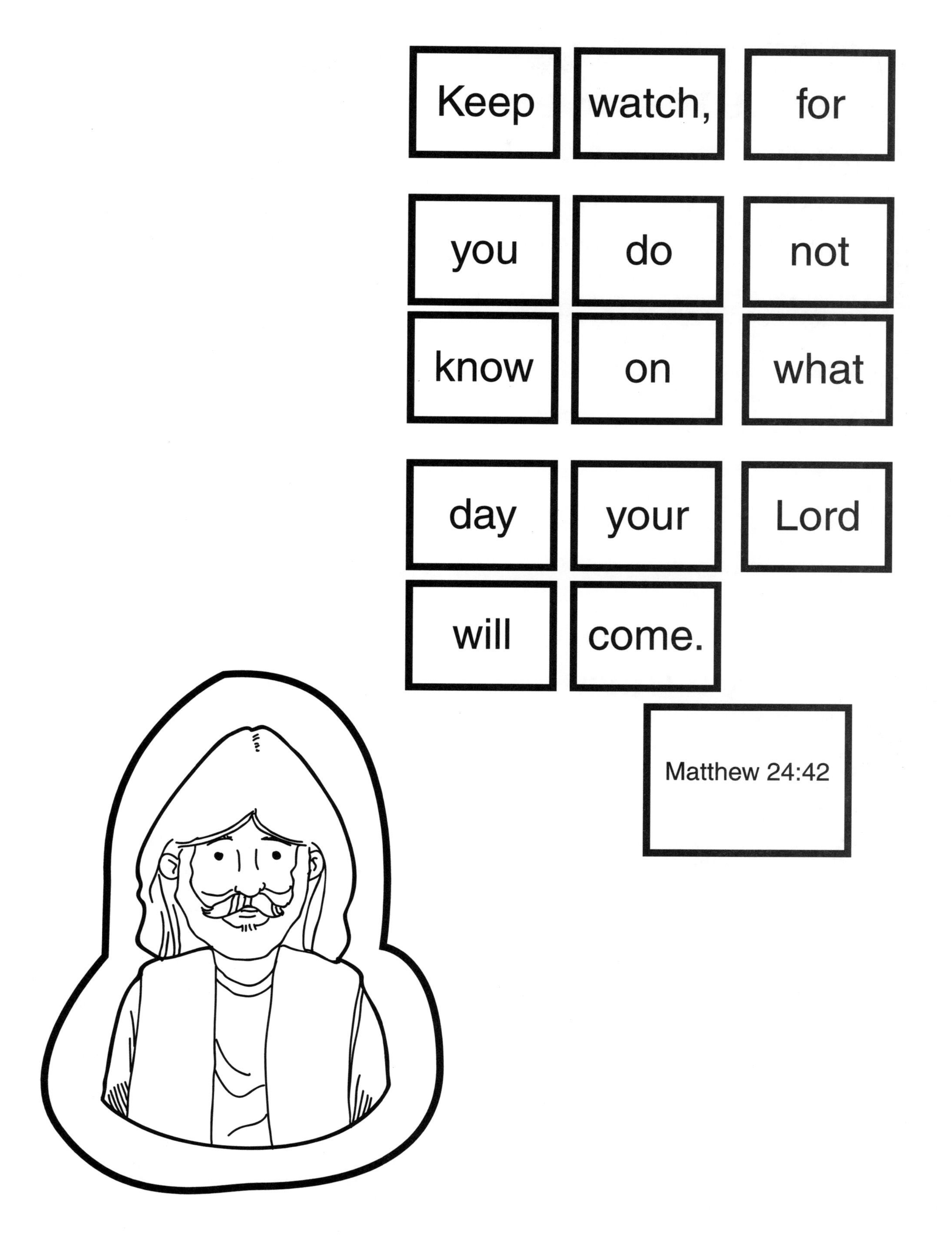
Keep
watch,
for
you
do
not
know
on
what
day
your
Lord
will
come.
Matthew 24:42

When's He Coming?

Creating and singing this song will create an awareness of the return of Jesus and our responsibility to be ready.

What You Need

- ⇨ song covers and word blocks from page 79
- ⇨ small paper plates
- ⇨ scissors
- ⇨ glue
- ⇨ hole punch
- ⇨ yarn
- ⇨ markers

Before Class

Duplicate the song cover and word blocks from page 79. You will need six paper plates per child. Make a sample song book to sing before introducing the craft.

What To Do

1. Give the students the song covers and word blocks to cut out.
2. Allow the children to color the song cover.
3. Instruct the children to glue the cover and blocks to one paper plate each.
4. Assist in punching holes in paper plates and tying together with yarn.

SAY

Even though I don't know when Jesus is coming back, I want to be ready. Do you? How many of you know your sins are forgiven? Do any of you want to ask Jesus to get your heart ready for His return?

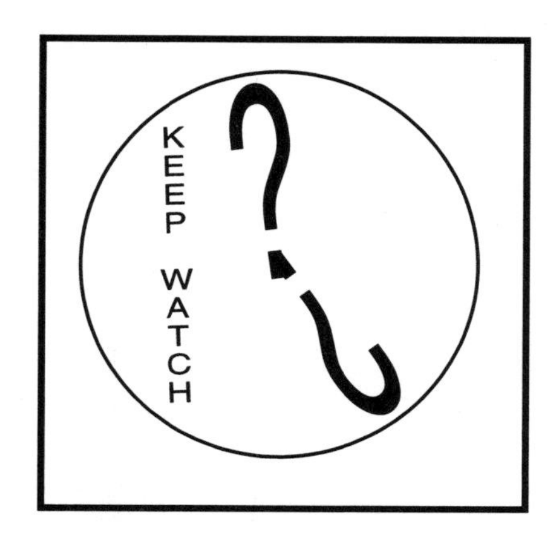

Sing to the tune of "Are You Sleeping"

When's He coming?
When's He coming?

I want to be ready.

Watching for His coming.

Self Worth

Memory Verse

Let the little children come to me.

~Matthew 19:14

Each One Is Special

Based on Mark 9:33-37, 10:13-16

Jesus loved children. He was busy teaching when a group of women came with their sons and daughters. "Bless my child, please," begged one.

"Mine, too," asked another.

Jesus looked down with a smile and reached down to pick up one of the children. Then He heard the disciples.

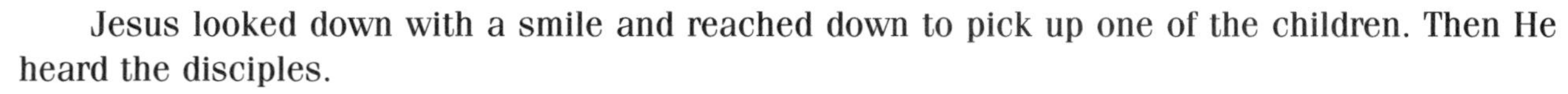

"What are you barging in for?" asked Andrew.

"Yes, Jesus is teaching us," said Philip.

"Hurry, take your children and get out of our way," Peter told them.

"Andrew," Jesus said sharply. At His tone, the others turned and looked at Jesus. "Do not keep the children away from me. I love each one of them. They are all precious in the sight of God...just as precious as you, Andrew, and you, Peter, and all the rest."

Jesus' words had silenced the disciples but they were far from happy. That didn't stop Jesus from taking time with each of the children. He hugged them, blessed them, smiled and listened to their stories. They were important to Him.

Another time the disciples asked Jesus which one would be the most important in the kingdom of heaven. Some of them were saying Peter, others John.

Jesus turned to a child nearby and called to him, "Child, come here."

Jesus picked up the child and held him on His knee. "Do you see this child?" He asked. "Anyone who enters heaven as this little child — trusting and humble — that is who will be the greatest in God's kingdom."

The disciples looked at each other, but Jesus wasn't finished. "And anyone who loves a child and teaches him or her about Me makes God happy. If you hurt a child or neglect to teach him or her about Me you will be in trouble. It would be better if a large stone were tied about your neck and you were thrown into the water."

The disciples were silent as they heard what Jesus said. They heard Him speak softly to the child, "You are important to God, and very precious. He loves you. He loves every child."

For Discussion

How important are you to God? Are you as important as the pastor? As your father? As I am?

I'm Special Sun Catcher

When the sun comes shining through this sun catcher, it will remind your students that they are special...to you and to God.

What You Need

- ⇨ stained glass circle from page 82
- ⇨ small paper plates
- ⇨ permanent markers
- ⇨ scissors
- ⇨ fishing line
- ⇨ clear transparency sheets
- ⇨ hole punch

Before Class

Duplicate the stained glass circle from page 82 to transparencies. Make a sample craft and hang it where the students will see it as they walk in the classroom.

What To Do

1. Give each child a stained glass circle to cut out and color with permanent markers. Instruct the children to not leave any clear transparency showing.
2. Assist in cutting the center from a paper plate.
3. Show how to glue the stained glass to the plate circle.
4. Encourage the students to write the memory verse around the edge of the plate "frame."
4. Have the students punch a hole in the top of the plate. Assist in tying fishing line in the hole for a hanger.

SAY

There's someone in this room who thinks each of you is special. I do! (Child's name) is special because he is good at memorizing the memory verse. (Child's name) is special because she is always at Sunday school on time. (Name each child and why he or she is special.) But more important than what I think, God thinks you are special...and God is always right!

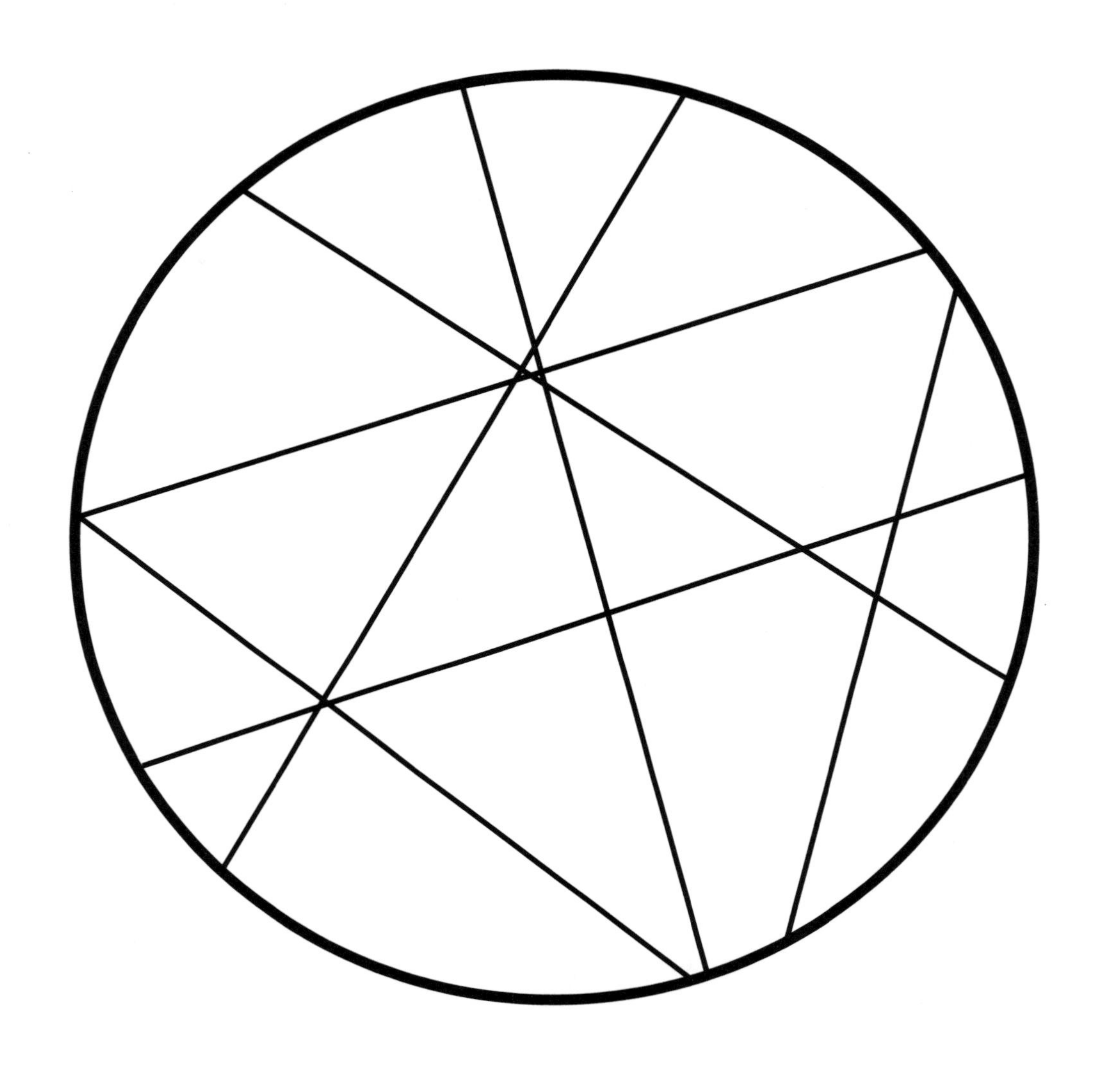

The Children's Windsock

The children will enjoy making this windsock to remind them they are special to God.

What You Need

- ⇨ children's and Jesus' faces from page 84
- ⇨ paper plates
- ⇨ scissors
- ⇨ crayons
- ⇨ stapler
- ⇨ hole punch
- ⇨ yarn
- ⇨ glue
- ⇨ crepe paper (four colors)

Before Class

Duplicate the faces from page 84. Make a sample windsock to decorate the classroom.

What To Do

1. Give each child the duplicated faces to color and cut out.
2. Instruct the children to glue the picture of Jesus to the middle of the plate, then glue the children's faces around it. They should also write the memory verse on the plate.
3. Instruct the children to punch a hole at the top of the plate. Assist in tying yarn through the hole for a hanger.
4. Have each child cut four lengths of crepe paper from the different colors. Assist in stapling the crepe paper to the bottom of the plate. Cover the staple backs with tape to avoid injury.

SAY

Won't it be fun to watch the tails of the windsock fly? When you see the tails fluttering, look up to the face of Jesus and remember: He loves you. You are special to Him!

Trust

Memory Verse

You will keep him in perfect peace.

~Isaiah 26:3
NKJV

Wake Up, Jesus

Based on Matthew 8:23-27

Jesus was tired. He had been preaching and healing the sick all day. "Let's cross over to the other side of the lake," He said to His disciples.

As the small fishing boat rocked gently on the blue waves, Jesus went to the back of the boat, found a pillow for His head, and fell sound asleep.

All of a sudden, a fierce storm blew over the sea. The wind screamed and whipped around the boat. The waves crashed against the sides of the boat and water splattered inside.

The disciples were terrified. "As a fisherman I've seen many storms, but I've never been in one this violent," said Peter.

"The boat is going to sink," said Andrew.

"Where's Jesus?" asked James. "Why doesn't He help us?"

"Jesus!" called Thomas. "Don't You care that we are going to die in this storm?"

"Save us, Jesus," shouted John over the noise of the wind and waves.

Jesus sat up and looked at the storm. "Why are you afraid?" He asked the disciples.

Surprised, the disciples watched as the waves beat on the boat. "Because we are going to die," they wanted to say, but Jesus was speaking again. "Why is your faith so small?"

Then Jesus stood, held out His hand and said in a quiet yet commanding voice, "Peace, be still."

Immediately, the wind stopped and the boat started rocking gently in the calm waters.

"Why don't you trust Me?" Jesus asked the disciples.

The disciples looked at each other in surprise. "How great Jesus is! Even the wind and the waves obey His voice!"

For Discussion

1. Are you afraid in the dark or in a storm?

2. Who is with you even if you are alone?

Peaceful Waters

Coloring peaceful waters will remind your students that just as Jesus calmed the storm and brought peace to His disciples, He can give them peace when they are afraid.

What You Need

- ⇨ boats and verses from page 87
- ⇨ small paper plates
- ⇨ craft stick
- ⇨ crayons
- ⇨ scissors
- ⇨ glue

Before Class

Duplicate the boat and verse from page 87 for each child. Make a sample craft to use in telling the story.

What To Do

1. Give each student a boat to color and cut out. Have them glue the craft stick to the back of the boat, extending from the bottom.
2. Instruct the children to color the paper plate to look like water with peaceful waves.
3. Help the children fold the plate so there is a 1" space in the middle.
4. Cut a slit in the middle space for the craft stick. Allow the children to open the plate again then push the end of the craft stick through the slit until the boat sits on the water.
5. Give the students a verse to cut out and glue to the middle of the waves.

SAY

The water looks calm, doesn't it? But just minutes before Jesus calmed the waters, the disciples were hanging on, fearful they were drowning. All they had to do was ask Jesus for help. When your heart is afraid, ask Jesus for peace.

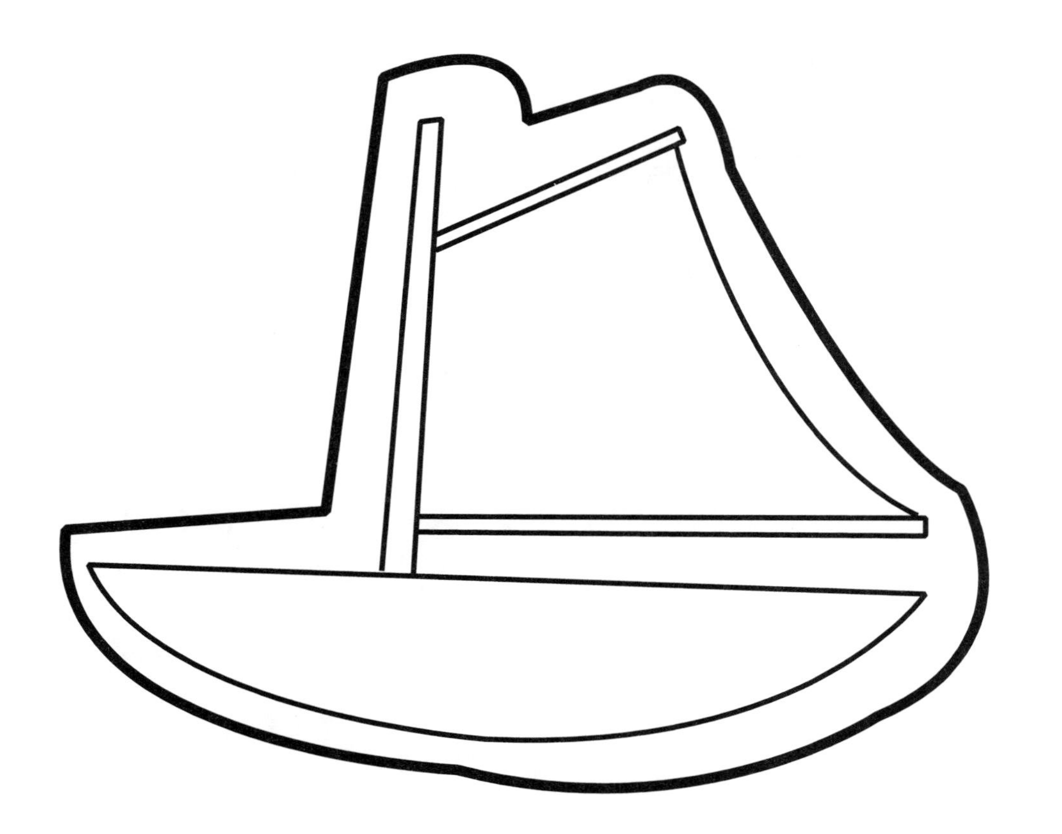

You will keep

him in

perfect peace.

Isaiah 26:3

NKJV

Raindrops Are Falling

This prayer box will help your students to pray for their classmates, and remind them to have faith to believe their prayers will be answered.

What You Need

⇨ umbrella and raindrops from pages 89 and 90

⇨ 9" paper plates

⇨ crayons

⇨ stapler

⇨ tape

⇨ chenille stems

Before Class

Duplicate the umbrella and raindrops from pages 89 and 90 for each child. Make a sample umbrella so the children can see the finished craft.

What To Do

1. Allow the children to decorate the umbrella.
2. Demonstrate how to staple the umbrella to a paper plate. Cover the staples with tape to avoid injury.
3. Instruct the children to bend one end of a chenille stem for a handle and tape it inside the umbrella.
4. Give the children a verse raindrop to cut out. The raindrops can be stored inside the umbrella.
5. Instruct the children to turn over the raindrops and see who can put them in order first.

SAY We are all afraid sometimes. I sometimes am afraid of (name something). But when I am afraid, I like to repeat this verse to myself. It reminds me to trust in God. Why don't you try it when you are afraid?

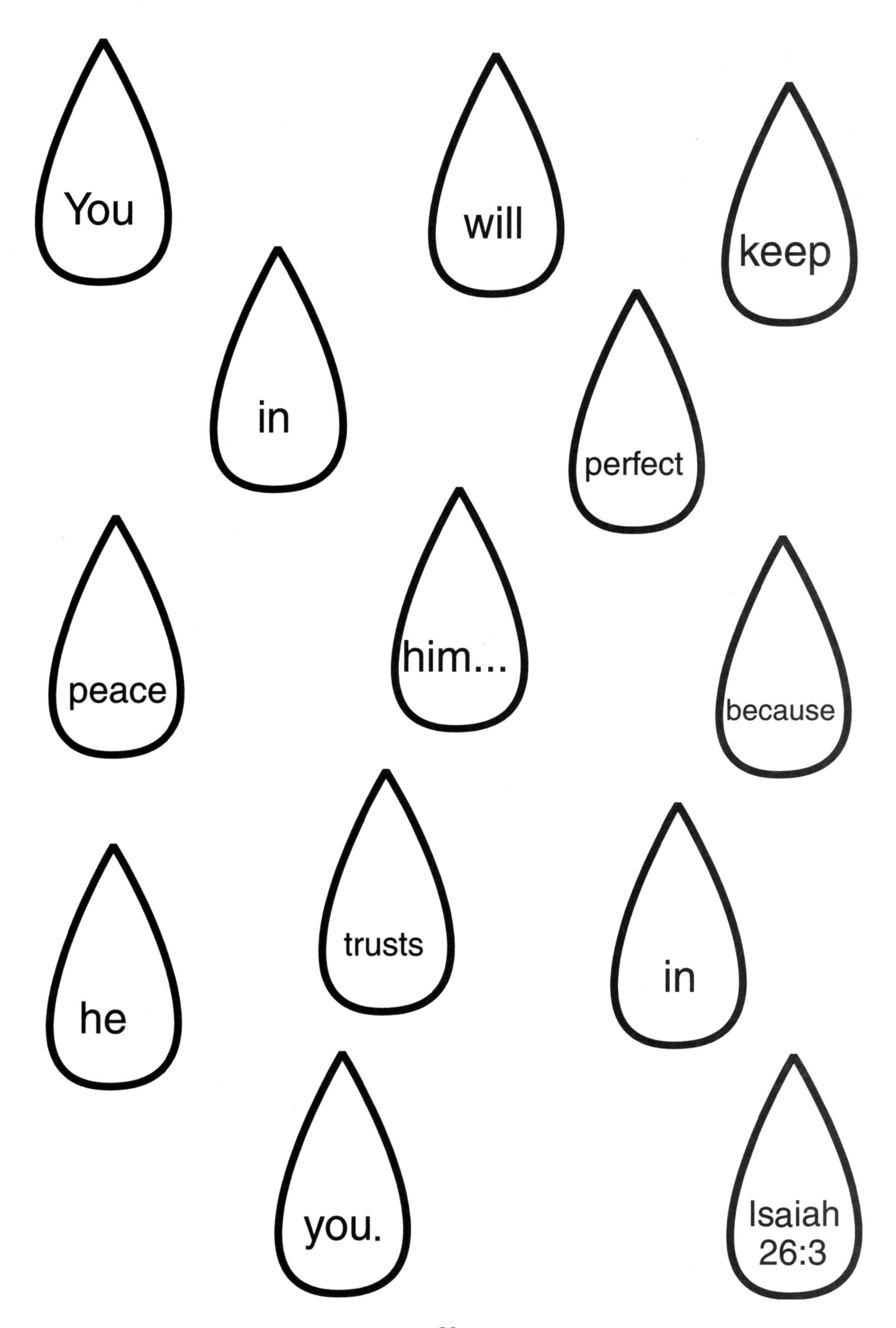
You
will
keep
in
perfect
peace
him...
because
he
trusts
in
you.
Isaiah
26:3

Wisdom

Memory Verse

Blessed is the man who finds wisdom.
~Proverbs 3:13

King Solomon's One Wish

Based on 1 Kings 3

After King David died, Solomon, his son, became the new king of Israel. One night God appeared to him in a dream saying, "Ask Me for whatever you wish, and I will give it to you."

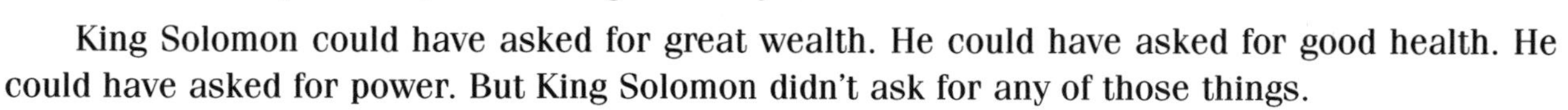

King Solomon could have asked for great wealth. He could have asked for good health. He could have asked for power. But King Solomon didn't ask for any of those things.

"Lord, You have made me king over Your people," he said. "I am young, I don't know how to be a king to these people. Lord, I ask You for wisdom."

Solomon's reasoning pleased the Lord. "Because you have not asked for long life, for great wealth, nor power, I will give you your wish. You shall have a wise and understanding heart if you will obey My laws. I will also give you riches and honor."

Not long afterward, two mothers came to King Solomon. The women lived in the same house and were holding babies in their arms. One lady was holding a baby that had died, the other was holding a living baby.

"King Solomon," cried the one. "It is her baby who died. I know my own child."

"No, no!" insisted the other. "My baby is alive. She stole my baby while I slept."

Solomon called for his sword and told the guard, "Cut the living baby in two. Then give half to one woman and half to the other."

The first mother said, "Yes, wise King Solomon, cut him in two so that neither of us will have him."

But the other mother screamed in horror. "No! Please don't hurt the baby. Give the baby to her. At least he'll live."

By this King Solomon knew who the true mother was. A true mother would not want her child to be harmed. Only God could have given King Solomon this wisdom. All the people who heard of his wisdom respected their new king.

For Discussion

If you were given the chance to have one thing you wanted, what would you ask for?

A Happy Baby

As the children concentrate on placing a happy baby in the cradle, they will learn that we make others happy when we are wise.

What You Need

- ⇨ patterns from page 93
- ⇨ paper plates
- ⇨ pastel felt
- ⇨ scissors
- ⇨ crayons
- ⇨ glue
- ⇨ baby lotion

Before Class

Duplicate the patterns from page 93 for each child. Cut the pastel felt into 2" x 3" rectangles, one per child.

What To Do

1. Give each child a felt rectangle. Pour a small amount of baby lotion in the child's hand and demonstrate how to rub the lotion on the felt (the children enjoy the lotion and it will make the blanket smell like a baby).
2. Give each child a pattern page to cut out.
3. Give each child a paper plate and demonstrate how to trace the cradle onto the paper plate and cut it out.
4. Allow the children to color the cradle.
5. Instruct the children to color the baby and cut it out. Show the children where to glue the baby and blanket to cradle.
6. Write or have the children write the memory verse on the back of each cradle.

SAY

By asking God for wisdom, Solomon was able to save a baby's life. Do you think the baby's mother was happy? Do you think Solomon was happy to make the right decision? Our memory verse tells us we will be happy if we find wisdom. We will make others happy, too.

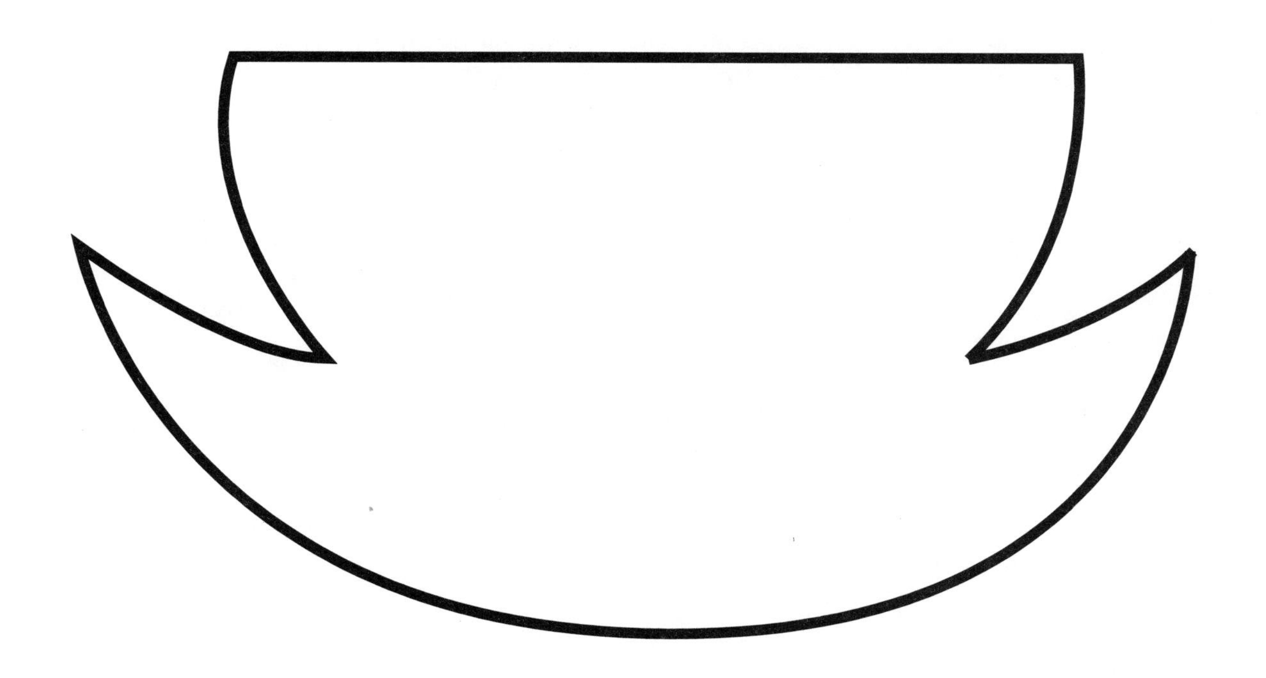

Solomon's Crown

As the children create their own crowns, they will be reminded to look to God for wisdom.

What You Need

- ⇨ patterns from page 95
- ⇨ paper plates
- ⇨ scissors
- ⇨ crayons
- ⇨ glitter
- ⇨ glue
- ⇨ cotton swabs

Before Class

Duplicate the patterns from page 95. Following the directions draw the cut lines on the inside of a paper plate for each child. Prepare a sample crown and wear it as you tell the story of Solomon.

What To Do

1. Give each child a paper plate and a page of jewels.
2. Demonstrate how to cut on the lines of the plate. Help those who need assistance.
3. Instruct the children to color and cut out the jewels.
4. Show how to glue the jewels to the plate.
5. Allow the children to use cotton swabs to spread glue on the jewels and sprinkle glitter over the glue.

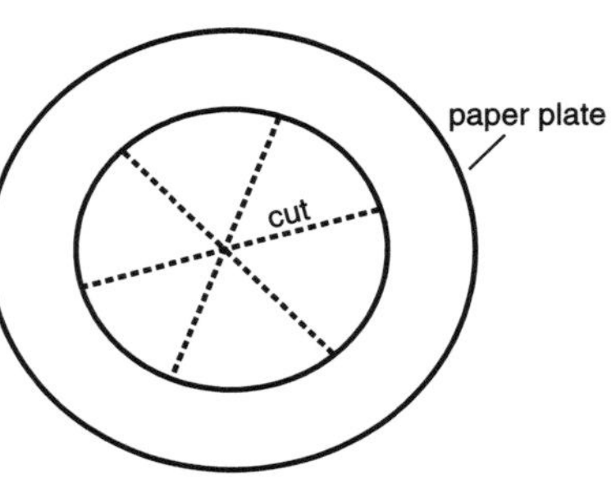

SAY

Solomon was king but he still needed wisdom from God. Solomon could not face his kingdom without God's wisdom. Each of us needs wisdom from God to face each day.

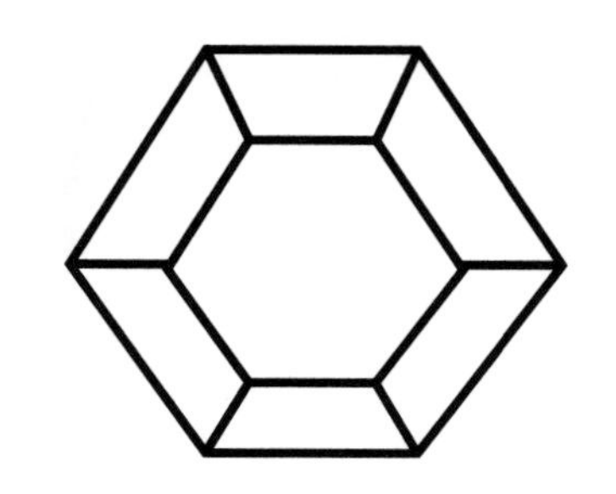
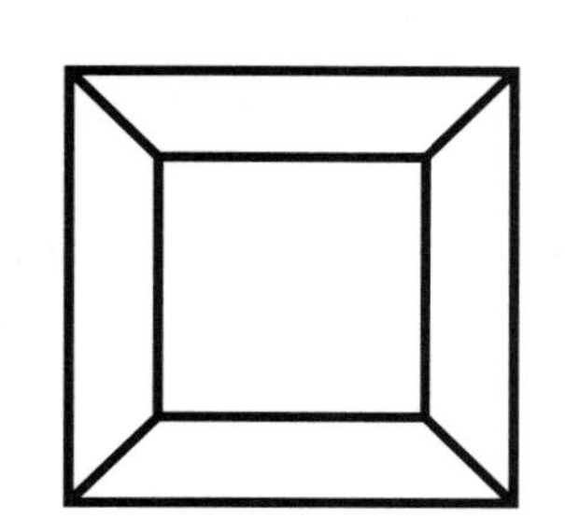
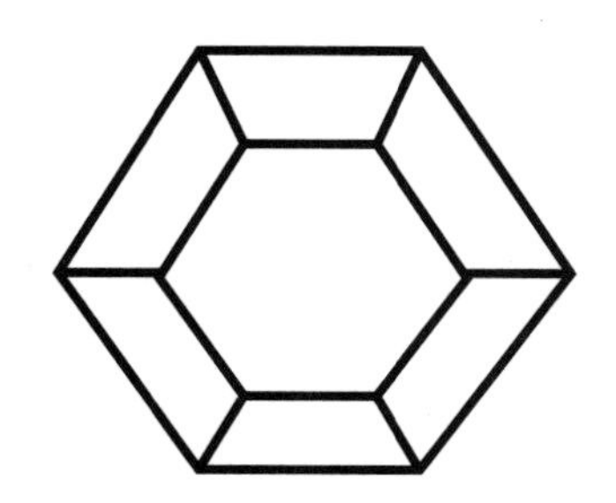
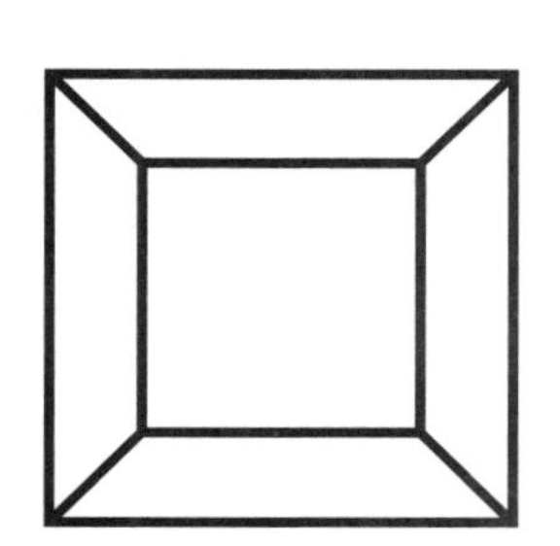
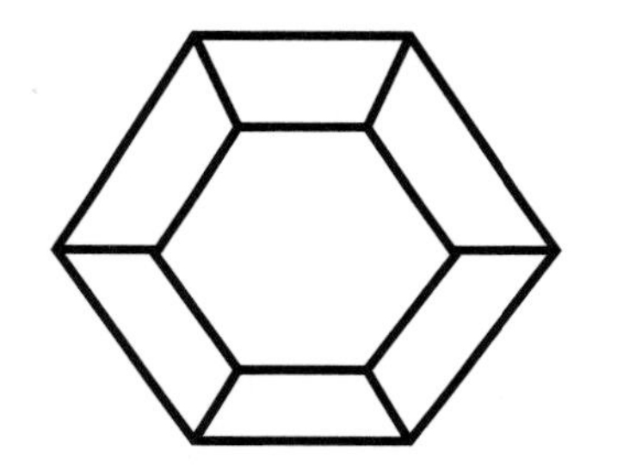
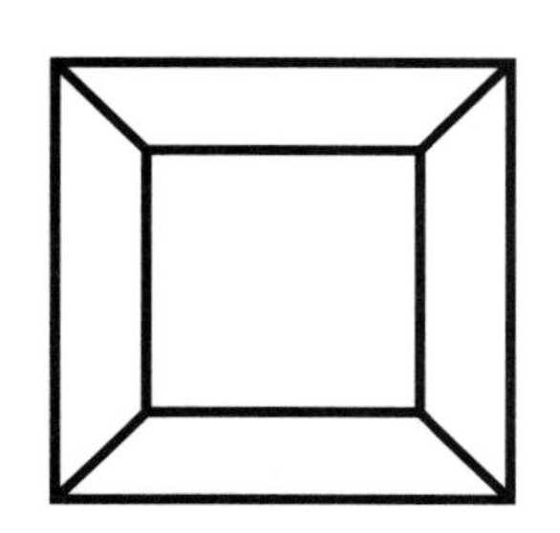
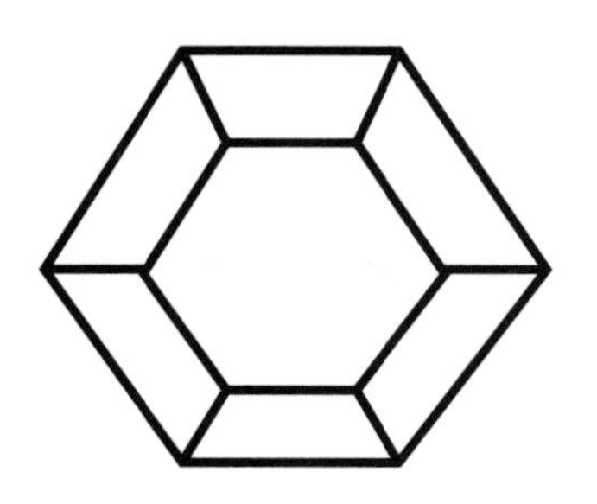
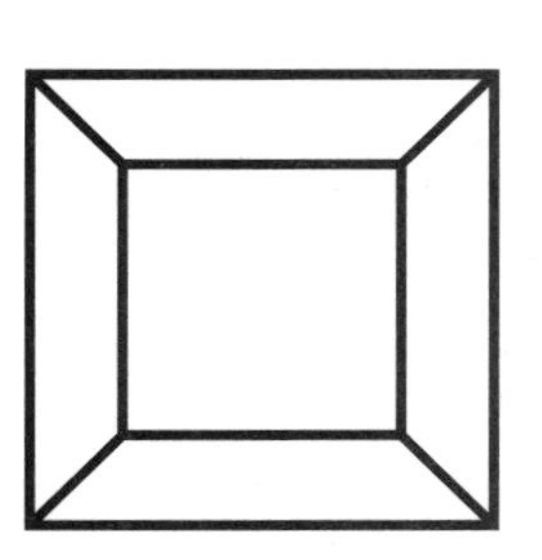
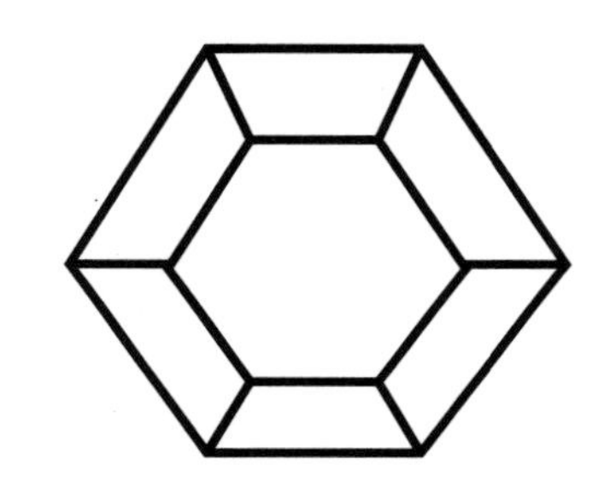
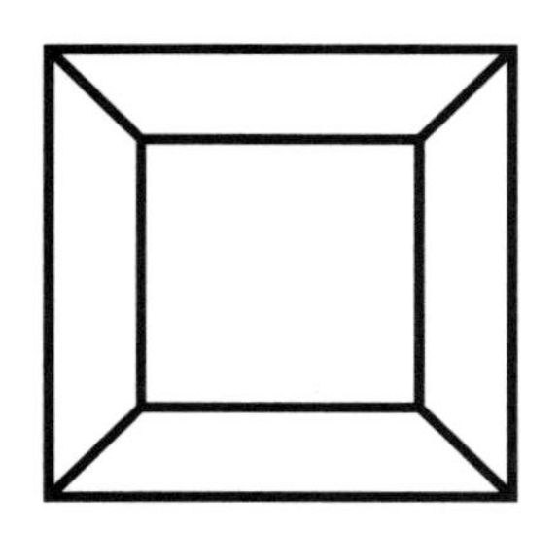